Ghost Notes

Art Edwards

Defunct
Press

Published by Defunct Press
www.defunctpress.com

Copyright ©2007 Art Edwards
www.artedwards.com

The author asserts the moral right to be identified as the author of this work.

ISBN-13: 978-0-9799066-1-9
ISBN-10: 0-9799066-1-X

1 2 3 4 5 6 7 8 9 10

Cover photograph by Daryl Thetford
www.thetfordphotography.com

We'll pass oranges with our necks just like *Charade*,

And with our drinks we'll all make lemonade.

—"Riverboat Captain"

Ghost Notes

October 1995
Wednesday

Journey: Escape

I'm sitting in my hotel room in San Paolo, Orange County, California. I'm in bed, the sheet pulled over my legs, my back against the wall-mounted headrest. It's the middle of the day. The television plays scenes without volume, but I'm not paying attention. I'm thinking about the speed of life, how fast you can move and still get nowhere. Nebraska to Cali in a week, a gig and a bad meal and a La Quinta Inn every night. Three days ago I was in the desert. Utah, mesas, gold flowers along the freeway. California's a desert, too. Don't let the palm trees fool you.

The telephone rings, an abrasive tone that startles me a little. I know better than to hope it's Celia. I put the receiver to my ear. "Hello."

"HOTE," comes the voice from the other end. It's Fife, our road manager. He sounds worked up, like he just had to prove someone wrong.

"Yeah, Fife," I say. "What's up?"

"Soundcheck's up," he says. His voice sounds rough from too many cigarettes, a habit he indulges only on the road. Several people on the bus have a habit—usually a bad habit—they yield to on tour, and Fife's is smoking cigarettes. Forrest smokes pot. Wally and Remeny collect porn. Mine is staying in my hotel room. I don't go out, don't answer the door. "I had to butt heads with Evermore to get them going," Fife says.

"What did they do?" I ask. I always want to be a fly-on-the-wall for these backstage arguments. I want to know what goes on behind the scenes of a rock band, to know the intimate details of a rock tour, even though I'm in a rock band and in the middle of a rock tour. When people ask me what goes on, what happens backstage or on the tour bus or back at the hotel, I have no idea what to tell them. I shy away from telling them the truth, that the band members avoid each other, that we sleep a great deal and watch too much TV, that we're more or less going through the motions out here. Instead, when asked, I roll my eyes and act like there's something extremely interesting going on that I can't tell them. I get the impression this is the best answer to give, that it's the right answer, even though it's not the truth. I can't figure out how to live my life the other way, where the best answer *is* the truth.

"They soundchecked twenty minutes late," Fife says. "And then they acted like they could just slide right into our slot. I put an end to that right there. I told Devin, 'The contract says—'"

"Okay," I say, regretting I asked. "What time do you need me there?"

"A.S.A.F.P.," he says, and I hear him take a drag from his cigarette. Fife holds a cigarette strangely, not between his fingers but between his finger and thumb, so it points back towards him, and when I'm around him I have to fight the urge to take the cigarette and put it back the right way. "They're putting your equipment on the stage right now."

"Okay," I say. "I'll be there."

"Right now," he says and hangs up.

I hang up the phone. *Right now.* He says it with such conviction, like nothing in the world could top it. Tell you what, Fife. I'll trade you right now for just about anything.

Walking out of my hotel room, the sun hits me like the pop of a flash bulb. Southern California. Celia and I vacationed close to here once, in San Diego, a sort of belated honeymoon. We rented a bungalow on the beach and spent ten days roaming the coast. We were both drunk with the idea of relocating here. We scoured neighborhoods, checked out real estate. We wondered how many records the band would have to sell for the dream to come true. Of course, that kind of money never trickled down to me, but back then it was all still in front of us, the dice in mid-roll, our future one giant possibility.

The sidewalk runs along Main Street, where manicured lawns and parking lots lead to superstores. Office Plus, Dart Mart, Home Makeover. Fun Yung Moon have played here before, a thousand-seater called the Equinox. The last time, two years ago, the club oversold tickets; they had to remove tables to accommodate all the people. After a two-hour set with non-stop crowd surfing and three encores, we signed autographs. The kids' faces glowed with sweat and hero-worship. One offered up his cheerleader sister to any band member who would come back to his house and party with him. "No, thanks," I said, struggling to sign something that looked like "Houy" on the back of his shirt.

Prospects for tonight's show are not so good. We tour with a band called Evermore. Evermore's debut record came rushing out of the gate last month, MTV Buzz Bin, number two Heat Seekers. Glen, our manager, fought like hell to get the two bands on the same bill. He argued that Fun Yung Moon, a platinum-selling band with its follow-up ready to go, touring with Evermore, the next big thing, would ensure a packed house at every stop. But neither band has held up its end of the bargain. Evermore faded almost as quickly as they blossomed, and our new record, *Fun Yung-Ola*, gets little radio play in Orange County, or anywhere else. Turnout is expected to be less than half-capacity.

"Kids forget fast," Glen told me. I stopped by his office when the band played Los Angeles. Glen's office, the whole top floor of a white-brick building just off Sunset, feels like Command Central of the music business. Everyone touches base with him. The manager of Smashing Pumpkins, REM's A&R guy, Iggy Pop, you never knew who might stumble in. "Of course, it would've helped if you guys hadn't made a country record to follow up a rock record."

"Don't blame me for that one," I said. "I don't even like country."

"Ah, the music business," Glen said with a wry smile. He sat back in his chair, put his hands behind his curly bush of red hair. "Everyone takes responsibility for the success, and they can't dish it off fast enough when there's a failure. I wish I had a dime for every band I've managed who blamed someone else for their mistakes."

Glen's notoriously cutthroat with his bands. He makes twenty percent of everything Fun Yung Moon brings through the door, plus we pay his office expenses. "You *do* have a dime for every band you've managed," I said.

"Hey, you're right," Glen said, brightening. "A dime and then some."

I walk up a worn path that leads to the Equinox, bracing myself. I get no satisfaction from these gigs anymore. I remember how important they felt when we first started, Lance's drumming a little ahead of the beat, Gad and Verge doing their thing on guitar, the crowd going bonkers. I thought the music would lead us somewhere. I didn't know to where, but I believed nothing that felt so good could lead to anyplace too far off the mark.

Now I feel like a traitor. It kills me to think that the band has become just another job to me. *So, Hote. You've finally hit the big time and—What? You don't want it? Are you insane? Isn't this exactly what you've always dreamt of? If not this, then what?* It's starting to sound like complete bullshit, even to me.

The Equinox parking lot, which will teem with cars and people tonight, is vacant now, save a lone basketball hoop at the far end. The muffled sounds of musical instruments come from inside, Gad's and Verge's guitars. I don't want to go in yet. The rest of the band will be in full soundcheck mode, and I'll just stand there, my bass strapped over my shoulder, listening to the strumming, the thumping, the feedback going on all around me, not believing that every sound could be so out-of-synch with every other sound, each voice and thump and note in the middle of its own repetitive, boring song. I try to make the sounds match up in my head but they're too discordant, music that is un-musicable.

The wood-shingled roof of the Equinox comes almost to the ground, with a cut-out that leads to the backstage door. I have to remember, tomorrow's a day off. I love days off on the road the way others in the band love trips to the strip club or nights out on the record company. They're my days to realign, to regroup. I can do whatever I want, or I can do nothing, just sit in my hotel room and watch the day go by. I would've gone crazy without them these past few years. Just get through the gig. Tomorrow's all yours. I push my way through the backstage door.

"I can't hear it," Gad screams from center stage.

What is it with guitar players? They play the loudest, most direct-sounding instrument in the history of the world and yet they can never hear it. Everyone else in the band can be plugging their ears, audiences can leave in frustration, sound engineers can take everything else out of the mix, but the guitar player still can't hear it. Gad can never hear it.

Gad looks quizzically at his amplifier, his ass-length blond hair falling into his face. His hair's never been cut, as far as I can tell, the tightly curled metal 'do of five years ago growing more chaotic with every passing year. It's now this long, frizzy mutation that's forever getting stuck to his cheeks or under his guitar strap. His elbows and knees suggest the angles of a stick figure, and this, combined with his hair, makes him look like a scarecrow, or a tall, hysterical woman.

Gad strums a few chords, holds the guitar neck with one hand, grabs the amp with the other and wiggles it a half-inch closer to the front of the stage. He strums his guitar again, adjusts one of the amplifier's knobs. Strums.

"Don't worry about it," comes a voice, seemingly out of nowhere. It's Addie, our sound engineer, speaking through a microphone from behind the soundboard. "I'll put some rhythm guitar in your monitor. You won't notice the difference."

Gad doesn't move. He wants to solve this problem himself. He strums his guitar again, looks at his amplifier. Strums, looks.

Forrest plays hacky-sack behind his drum kit. Solid and stocky, Forrest went to Arizona State on a track and field scholarship, but he dropped out when he realized he could make more money playing in local bands. He plays drums with the same precision he does everything, attentive as a machine, minding the beat with a focus he seems hard-wired for. It's the same way he plays hacky-sack now, keeping the ball in the air with kicks and stops and caroms that suggest neither effort nor ease. I've always liked Forrest, but I hated it when the band voted to throw out Lance, right before we signed our record deal.

We figured it would be best coming from me, "most effective," Gad said, hearing it from his best friend since high school, his rhythm section partner in three previous bands. Gad and Verge waited outside the practice room while I broke the news.

Lance was stunned at first, his large frame rigid behind his drum kit, but his surprise quickly melted into relief. He was glad, he said. He was going to tell his parents right away, to get it behind him as soon as possible. He told me I shouldn't feel bad, that he would've eventually killed Gad. "I don't envy you," he said. Lance bought a Jacuzzi with the severance money the band paid him, and I thought that was as perfect an ending as I could've hoped for.

But it didn't go away.

Forrest sees me come in. He catches the hacky-sack and, with nothing but a raise of his eyebrows, offers to include me in the game. No. I have to get ready.

"Hote," Fife calls from the back of the club. "Phone call."

"For me?"

"Take it at the back bar."

Behind the bar, spigots of a dozen or so bottles are covered with one long piece of plastic wrap. No club employees are around. Fife's briefcase sits on a bar stool. I pick up the phone, push the blinking white button.

"Hello."

"Josh?"

"Celia." A relief washes over me more powerful than medicine. Her whole person comes to me through that simple vibration, the sound of her voice. I can see her, blond hair, cell phone, in a business suit that draws looks as she walks by. How long has it been?

"Hi," she says.

"Hey."

"I'm sorry to bother you," she says. "I didn't have the itinerary so I had to call the club."

"It's okay. You're not bothering me."

"Good," she says. "Josh, I called because I have to—I have a question to ask you."

"Okay," I say. "But you don't need a reason to call me."

"Right," she says. There's an audible crack in the silence. She's usually so easy with her words, but this Celia sounds different. Each word starts at the bottoms of her feet and travels up through her body to her mouth. It might be because she's at work, people around, or it might be something else. "What I have to ask you is–"

"Yeah?"

"While you've been on the road . . . have you ever slept with someone else?"

"What?" This is strange because our phone calls, when we bother to talk at all, usually follow a predictable pattern of "Hello" and "How are you" and "That's interesting" and "I love you." She has her life in Phoenix, and I have mine out here on the road. Never the twain do meet. "You're asking me if I've ever slept with someone else?"

"I'm sorry," she says. "I'm not good at this. This is new for me."

My legs grow stiff, unnaturally stiff, like they've transformed into stone. Something's coming. I think briefly of hanging up and going back to soundcheck, hoping I miss it somehow.

"What kind of a crowd are you expecting tonight?" Celia asks.

"The usual," I say, taking the change in mood to adjust my legs. "Celia, why did you ask me if I've ever slept with someone else?"

"Because—" she starts, but stops herself. "I wish I could tell you not to be mad."

"Mad about what?"

"Just tell me, Josh," she says. "Have you? Tell me you have."

The rigor mortis returns, accompanied by a gnawing sensation. *She slept around on me.* "I haven't," I say, and I'm telling the truth. The much more damning question, how often did I *want* to sleep with someone else, doesn't come up, and I'm glad for it. It's a conversation I could never imagine having with her.

I hear her crying, hesitant weeps that don't sound right coming from her. Every tear admits defeat.

"Cel," I say. "Are you telling me you slept with someone else?"

Nothing but faint weeps.

I hang up the phone.

Boom. There it is. Just like that I'm back to square one, my life dropped like a bomb and left floating with the rest of the detritus. It was bound to happen, I guess. Everything took off too quickly not to correct with a vengeance. Fun Yung Moon went from a Tempe, Arizona nobody band to 2.6 million records sold. Celia went from complete stranger to wife. I moved from my mom's place in Ahwatukee to Seattle, to Lance's flophouse in Tempe, to our new home in the far, far suburbs of Phoenix. My path seems so random.

It could've worked out a million other ways, but it didn't. It worked out this way. So, who or what wanted it this way? Or, now that it isn't working, who do I complain to?

This news has a grip, and it shakes me, the first casualty in a long-expected war. I think briefly of sitting down on the floor, maybe crying, but I hear Verge playing his standard soundcheck lick, a pristine version of Digs Ven's "Piece of Luck." I'm next.

Fife sees me walk back into the room and hustles to reclaim his work place. I'm convinced I look different, that it shows, that people will notice the change in me. I can't let that happen. There's no one to trust out here.

"Nice of you to show up," Gad says, not looking up as he tunes his guitar.

That fuckhead. I should've expected it from him. The worse *Fun Yung-Ola* does on the charts, the more Gad takes it out on the rest of us. "Am I late?" I say, strapping on my bass. "Addie's still soundchecking Verge. That tells me I'm early."

Gad says nothing, continues tuning his guitar. He's recently switched from a Les Paul to a natural-wood Fender Telecaster in an effort to complete the country package he's trying to pull off. He's also taken to embroidered shirts, cowboy boots, and saying "howdy" and "y'all" whenever possible. No one else in the band is making the effort. Forrest always looks like he fell out of an undergrad class, workout shorts, T-shirt. Verge, in his stage get-up of fire-red suit coat and flared pants, could be a sideman for Elvis during the Vegas years. I wear gray slacks, a collared, aqua shirt, skater shoes. Much to Gad's dismay, the band looks like a mishmash of suburban tastes and rock 'n' roll affectations, which is probably all we ever were in the first place.

"Hote, let's hear you," Addie says.

I look down at my bass. What should I play? I usually search for some nugget to cheer me up during soundcheck, but I don't think I have it in me today. I rattle off the first thing that pops into my head, Rush's "Tom Sawyer," the low tones of my open E-string rumbling through the P.A.

Her work. That's probably what happened. Some suit at the magazine, a married editor with a BMW and specks of gray in his hair. It's amazing how much time she spends with her co-workers. Celia and I can go weeks without seeing each other, and she's with them all day, every day, eating lunch, planning projects, celebrating victories. It's more family-like than family, and that kind of presence is hard to compete with, especially when you're gone all the time, playing bass in Fun Yung Moon and, it's assumed, partying like a rock star.

But that party never comes for me. I'm not saying it couldn't— there have been plenty of opportunities to sample whatever the backstage room has to offer—but I never let it happen. Drugs, girls, I never pull the trigger. I always thought Celia and I transcended that kind of thing, that our marriage trumped it. I guess she didn't feel the same.

Forrest gives up his hacky-sack game for a chance to jam "Tom Sawyer." He climbs behind his drum kit and pounds out the beat with my bass line, making the rumble louder through the P.A. The thump of the bass drum and smack of the snare feel like an army coming up behind me, albeit an old army, good for a Memorial Day parade but probably not prepared for battle. Verge smiles around a cigarette. Wally, our road tech, shakes a devil-worshipping hand sign in the air. Even Fife makes an appearance, marching up to the lip of the stage.

"Thanks," Addie says, a signal for us to stop. "Now, let's hear the whole—"

"Wait a second," Fife says.

Everyone shuts up, and the band members take a few migratory steps towards Fife. We know this is where important decisions surface, tour plans unfurl, per diems get doled out. We've learned to both love and fear these moments the way cows both love and fear the approach of the farmer. We could be getting fed or branded. Either way, the moment holds our collective fate.

"There's been some confusion about the way the day's going to go from here," Fife says, "so let's clear that up. I need you all to check out of your hotel rooms so I can settle. That way we can be off to Fresno right after the show. Let's shoot to be out of here by–"

"Wait," I say, wondering if I missed something. "What are you talking about?"

Fife looks sheepish.

Gad looks nervous, too, but an upward tilt of his head suggests that he's in the right no matter what. He steps on his tuner, goes back to tuning his guitar. "We have a gig tomorrow in Fresno," he says. "The Harvest Festival. Tammy Wynette canceled. We're taking her place."

Fuck. The Harvest Festival? We played it last year, a party thrown by the City of Fresno to celebrate the end of harvest season. The people chomp on ears of corn and carry giant purple dogs won at the ring toss. The few kids who care about the band have to sit and watch from aluminum benches or risk getting kicked out. Most of the audience stays back, a million miles away. The Harvest Festival. It's a good paycheck, no doubt, but a gig with no soul.

"When did this happen?" I ask.

"Last night," Gad says. "Glen brought it to my attention, and I told him we'd do it. There are lots of country music fans in Fresno. I announced it at the beginning of soundcheck. You, of course, weren't here."

"It's our day off," I say. "We've got a week straight up the coast after this. Tomorrow's our last chance–"

"Tomorrow might be our last chance to get this record going," Gad says. "I don't know if you've noticed, Hote, but things aren't exactly swimming along."

"Isn't this a band decision?" I say. "This is something we used
to–"

"It's my decision," he says, looking at me. He doesn't look like
a scarecrow now. His eyes have a strange unevenness to them, one
bigger than the other. Johnny Rotten. "And I made it, *off*-off or no
off-off."

Someone chuckles—Wally, Remeny—I can't tell who. The joke's
on me. Long ago, as my sole contribution to the road life of Fun Yung
Moon, I asked that every day on tour without a gig is not just a day
off but a day *off*-off. That means we don't play, we don't travel, we
don't do interviews, nothing Fun Yung Moon from pillow to pillow.
Forrest and Verge rallied around me at the time, but interest in *off*-off
days has waned since then.

"Since when is everything your decision?" I say.

Gad takes a couple of steps towards me. "Since this record started
going south, and everybody else around here acts like it's party time
all the time," he says. "If you all want to play covers in Tempe for the
rest of your lives, go ahead. I'm turning this thing around, with or
without you. If you don't like it, there's the door."

I turn and look at the backstage door, the door I just walked
through on my way into the club. It looks strangely inviting, the
light of day shining through the cracks of its border, like everything
worthwhile sits just on the other side of it.

"That door?" I say, pointing to it.

Gad tunes his guitar again, but the wrinkles in his forehead say he
heard me and is not answering.

"So, all I have to do is walk out that door, and that's it?"

Everyone's frozen. Gad won't look up. Fife stares, bug-eyed.

"Well, Gad," I say. I pull the strap over my shoulder and set my
bass down. "Today, that's an offer I can't refuse." I walk through the
backstage door and out into the day, leaving nothing but silence
behind me.

Dale

Why am I standing in the burnt-brown backyard of my home in O.K. City, Oklahoma, west-looking? Is it because I know Sally and Josh are there? Is it because they're all I got left?

My buddy Von said he couldn't believe it when he saw Sally, carrying too many bags out of the Safeway, looking like she always did when she hurried, lips close together, eyes distracted, blond hair all mucked up. She was surprised to see him too, he said, about dropped all her groceries right there on the street. Von said they talked a little. What brought him to Phoenix, how long he'd been there, their families. "You didn't come up," Von said. Well, I'm not family. At least I don't think of myself as Sally's family. Husband? That was a long time ago. Father to Josh? Sure, but that can't matter much after all these years.

Still, she gave Von her address. He said he didn't even ask for it. "Let me give you my address," she said to him, and she went out of her way to set down all those things, find a pen, and write her house number down for him. Not her phone number but her house number. She must've wanted me to have it.

Every spring, Von and I go fishing in Utah. We hit a different lake every time, but we never find one we like. "Mormon-ville," Von called it the last time we were there. "There's more Mormons in Utah than anywhere."

"So, why do we come here?" I said.

He shrugged his shoulders, looked quizzically at the joint we'd been sharing. "You find as you get older you smoke more and enjoy it less?"

So, I told Von he might see me down in Arizona this year instead of up in Utah. "Never seen that part of the country," I said, Sally's address in front of me. I studied the curve of the numbers, the words *Euclid* and *Ahwatukee*. Great sounding secrets of words.

"Right," Von said. "You wanna see this part of the country. Whatever you say."

* * *

What most people think of as pain doesn't seem like pain at all to me. I'm not callous, although you'll find a few people who disagree. The truth is life has changed from the time we did the lindy-hop, drank at soda fountains and did chores for a few nickels. Life's gotten better, a *whole* lot better, for all of us, but that doesn't mean we can shake off the residue of the Old Pain. It doesn't mean we all move on to the New Pain. If you're from the Old Pain—the nastiness, beatings, "abuse" they'd call it now—you don't change because times change.

The pain of today, of "emotional distress," of "anxiety," of "depression," it's real, but it's not a belt across your back, or a baseball thrown at you from point-blank, or being tossed in a lake to learn how to swim. You learned how to swim or you drowned. My dad taught me how to swim that way. I learned, and I still haven't drowned.

I used tools to stay afloat. Joints. Smoothies. White crosses got me through the double-shifts. Quaaludes let me sleep. Those from the Old Pain find their solutions where they lie, not where they ought to lie.

I used to like to fight, back when fighting wouldn't land you in court. A good fight I looked forward to all week. It was harmless, a little dance you did with someone who needed to know the pecking order. "You gonna take a shot at my buddy?" Von said to this one factory guy who was sizing me up at the Bon Air. "Then take it. But if you do, cancel your dinner reservations, 'cause you're gonna need all night to kick his ass." I regret a lot of my past, but I don't regret the fights.

And the women back then, bad perms, menthol cigarettes, T-shirts from their husbands' underwear drawers. They all looked for a good way to pass the time, and I knew how to make the time pass in a good way. Other men—men not their husbands—had a distinct advantage. Marry them, and that pretty much guaranteed they'd never look at you again.

All except Sally. She had something the others didn't, the way she kept up her hair; the way she worked without knowing what she was doing, just knowing it needed to be done; the way she didn't let her eye wander. I thought, I could love this one.

We both worked at Willohby's, a restaurant just off the interstate on the Iowa side of the Mississippi. I was a cook, my first chance to flip burgers at a decent place. Sally waitressed. She could've easily blended in with the other waitresses, her accent and demeanor learned right there in the Midwest with the rest of them, but her looks elevated her. She didn't walk so much as shine her way into a room. Every time I saw her I'd hum, "Here Comes the Sun."

She knew it, too, how much I took to her. I'd let her catch me staring, saying with my eyes, *You're mine. I caught you. Make a sudden move and you'll see just how caught you are.* But she didn't come to me, like the rest. She didn't run away either. She went about her business, not speaking to me, not acknowledging capture. That silence, that balance between acceptance and rejection, drove me crazy. I started to hear her name in my sleep. I wandered out back to watch her pull away in her car at night. I was so careful not to touch her, other people noticed. Fran said, "Would you two just go to a drive-in and get it over with?"

One day, six weeks after I'd first seen her, I followed her down into the storage room. A lone light bulb lit the canned goods and cardboard boxes. I snuck up behind her and, without a word, touched her hair.

It startled her at first, her earrings shaking as she flipped around, but when she saw me she turned matter-of-fact. "Why aren't you away in the war?" she asked.

"Not everybody goes to the war," I said.

"Most everyone," she said. "You got kids?"

"No," I said. I laid the softest of kisses on her upper lip, but she didn't kiss back.

"My dad fought in World War II," she said.

"So did mine," I said. I kissed her again, and she kissed me back this time, wrapping her hands around my neck. I picked her up and set her on a stack of boxes that held cans of tomato juice.

"I love my dad," she said, kissing me.

"I hate mine," I said.

"Don't say that."

Finding out she was pregnant jerked me into the happiest moment of my life. There I was, as in love as I could be, and now Sally carried a little piece of me inside of her. I quit hanging out with my beer-drinking buddies. I drove Sally to and from work, even on my days off. I smiled so much the other cooks nicknamed me "Sunshine." Our path couldn't've been clearer. We got married that summer at City Hall, put a down payment on a house, and I took the first job offered me at the tractor factory.

But moments, they keep ticking away.

I soon realized that, because of the kid, Sally was mine. She couldn't go back to her parents' house, even if they would've let her. She couldn't take off on her own with a baby due. She had to stay with me in a way I hadn't noticed before, and I felt full possession of her. That's what started my mind wandering.

After work, I drove through downtown to get home, past Stan's, Vanderbeck's, the Bon Air. I had my first Smoothie, equal parts Schnapp's and whiskey, at the end of Sally's first trimester. It tasted deceitful, a strong, secret flavor that no one at home should know about. Most nights I stayed at the Bon Air until bedtime. If Sally called looking for me, I stayed longer.

Still, we probably could've weathered it if I'd stuck with Smoothies. This is the sixties we're talking about. It was a big world getting bigger.

Von and I drove into Capp Island, into the projects, drove right up the middle of them and waited for someone to come up to the car.

"What chu want?" the man said.

"What chu got?" I said.

His eyeballs scanned both ways. "Meet me 'round back," he said.

Von and I dropped our first hit downtown, in the Bon Air parking lot, watching each other put the tabs on our tongues. I disappeared soon after that, ran out of the tavern yelling, "My hair's on fire," or some shit. I don't remember much. I think I wandered around, searched for places where people couldn't find me, watched street lamps and neon signs and the tail lights of cars. I woke up the next morning in a stand of trees, the buzz of the freeway not far away. When I got home, Sally wouldn't speak to me.

She flicked on the front burner of the stove, slammed down a pan.

"How long's this gonna last?" I asked. I sat at the kitchen table, my head in my hands. I couldn't take the silence punctuated by the slams of the pan.

She scooped out a tablespoon of margarine and dropped it in, shook the pan like she might strangle it. "Is it ever gonna happen again?" she asked.

"What?" I said.

"Never again," she yelled, slamming the pan down.

But I couldn't stop. One hit became two hits, two became four. You don't forget the feel of it, yellow and red and green all around, the Old Pain annihilated. Hell. I didn't want to stop. My Friday nights became Sunday mornings, became Tuesday afternoons. I quit going to work, hung out at Prospect Park or in the alley behind the Bon Air. I could take just enough acid to be high at noon and coming down as I walked through the door at night. It worked for three weeks, until the first Friday of the month came.

"Did you get your paycheck?" Sally asked. She set places for us in the dining room, her round belly making it hard for her to bend over. Her parents had given us their old dining room set, and Sally wanted to eat off it.

"No paycheck this month," I said. I walked past her into the kitchen. I felt suffocated, my throat dry, my chest tight. I knew what was coming. I turned off the kitchen light and sat down.

"What?" she said. She came to the doorway. The light from the dining room silhouetted her, the frazzled blond hair, the maternity dress.

"No paycheck this month," I said.

"What do you mean, 'No paycheck this month'?" she said. She flicked the light on.

"Quit my job," I said.

"You quit your job?" she said.

"Quit my lousy job," I said.

I didn't look up at her, but I could feel her standing there, taking it all in. When Sally was surprised, her eyeballs bounced quickly rightleftrightleft, gears clicking, forging the information into a new tool. It was that power, the power behind that bouncing, that gave me no chance of escape. "But you worked all month," she said. "Where's your paycheck *this* month, Dale?"

She didn't talk to me for a long time after that. I wanted to ask her how long her silence would last, but I knew better. I'd crossed the line. The tightness in my throat and chest stayed. I couldn't eat, couldn't swallow. I left our house early in the morning and didn't come home until I knew she'd be asleep. I tried not to look at her because it would remind me of what I'd done, of how far I'd stepped outside her, *them*. I took the bus downtown most days, hung out in the alley behind the Bon Air.

Drugs kept Sally's silence at bay. They made noises in my head, words, flashes of light. I waited for Manny—he knew I'd be there—and bought from him whatever I could to usher me through the day. If I had no money, Manny would let me run an errand for him, take the bus up the hill to make a delivery. I'd come back and he'd have my freedom waiting for me in a little piece of aluminum foil.

But then came Josh, and I straightened up. Sally's parents somehow knew to find me at the Bon Air. They called me there, made Dex come into the alley to let me know. "You're kid's coming," he said. He turned to go back in as quickly as he'd come out.

"Where are they?" I asked. It was late morning. Manny hadn't arrived yet.

"Faith Lutheran," Dex said. The screen door slapped closed behind him.

I took off running. Faith Lutheran was a mile away, the last quarter-mile straight up a hill the track team used for training. I could be there in ten minutes. The flap of life went through me on that run, a rush that blew away anything I could get from Manny. I made the turn at Seventh Street thinking, I could be a new man, a new husband, a father to that kid. I'd never hang out behind the Bon Air ever again, never take drugs again. I took that last hill like it was nothing, consumed it with long strides. I made it through the automatic doors of the emergency room before I had to stop.

Sixteen hours later, the nurse let me in to see them. Sally was beautiful, a tired mess, her cheeks white as talcum. She mustered a smile for me. "Here he is," she said, her voice scratchy, holding him in the cradle of her arm. "Here's your son."

A good-lookin' kid too, right out of the womb, brown eyes, light brown hair, little puckered lips like his mother. I loved them both more than anything at that moment. Despite all my fuck-ups, I somehow hadn't been denied this family, this woman, this little bag of bones in my arms. I held my baby and cried. I wanted to be sober. The smallest chance to prove myself, and I'd do it. They'd all see. Even her parents, who'd refused to talk to me in the waiting room, would have us over to play Euchre on Friday nights.

I played second to Sally for as long as I could. I let her tell me what to do, what to pick up at the store, how much bleach to put in the laundry. It suited me for a while, but it couldn't last forever. I'm a man; I have to make money in this world. Sally's dad floated us for two months until I got another job at the tractor factory, this time in the shop, with benefits. I started to remember baseball and fishing and all the things I could teach Josh once he got older. The future looked fixed. I was Daddy, and I took it seriously.

But after a couple of months, Sally still wouldn't have a drink with me.

"I don't want one," she said.

"Whadya mean?" I said. "You used to love a drink. The kid's out cold."

"Not because of that," she said. We watched *Hogan's Heroes*. She stared at the TV with an eerie glow in her eyes, like something crawled around inside of them without her knowing. "I just don't want it."

I took the last tug of my gin and tonic. "So, you're done drinking," I said.

"I don't know," she said. "I don't want one right now. I know that."

"Goody two-shoes," I said, and I got up to make another.

She pulled her feet up underneath her. "If I want one you'll be the first to know," she said.

That house started to feel like a trap. Sally doting over the kid, formula on the stove, little stuffed animals Josh couldn't even see. It felt too . . . happy. The walls and ceiling kept all that happiness down and in. I battled it, parried it with my brain. I needed a place for the flip side of me, the lousy, sullen, rambunctious side. I pretended to watch TV, but I was looking for an escape.

The Bon Air. An occasional stop-by after work led to a trip every night, which led to a trip out back to see Manny. One Super Bowl Sunday I took too many mushrooms. When I got home, Sally was waiting up for me.

"Where have you been?" she said. She sat in the recliner with her arms crossed. The light from the lamp, on its dimmest setting, revealed shadows in her face.

I stood in the doorway, the door still open, the January cold rushing in behind me. I was fascinated by her face, the thinness of her neck, the way waves of heat came from the top of her head. I wanted to hug her, to feel that heat. "Von's," I said.

"Well, that's it," she said. "You won't come home here anymore if this is the state you come home in. This is a family, Dale. You'll understand that, or you won't be part of it."

"Sal," I said. I took a step or two towards her. "I can't—I can't do this right now."

"Dale, shut the damn door," she said, looking at me like the dumb ape I was.

I wanted my life with Sally and Josh, but I needed help to get through the day. Drugs made work life bearable. I laughed at the jokes of the other fellas. I laughed *at* the other fellas. I laughed at my job, which any trained monkey could've done. Drugs completely erased who I was, what I wanted, what I'd rather be doing. In ten months I never got caught, until that foil fell out of my pocket.

"Dale," my foreman said. "This yours?"

"Ha ha," I said.

"Dale, you on drugs here?"

"Drugs?" I said. "I don't do drugs."

"Dale, someone saw this fall out of your shirt pocket in the bathroom."

I couldn't do it, couldn't listen to him. I walked away. I walked out the back door of the shop, and I never went back.

It was clear, wasn't it? The world had no interest in me killing my Old Pain. Its only interest was keeping me down, keeping me rolling in it. It didn't matter one lick I felt otherwise.

That night after my last day of work I went to the Bon Air and drank Smoothie after Smoothie. I didn't know what would happen when I got home, but I knew I'd be numb for it.

And then it happened.

I was sorry for it later, but that doesn't matter. We all know it doesn't. Nothing I say can make it change. I've still got my Old Pain. I live with it, and let that be that.

She waited for me in the front room, in her nightie, curled up on the recliner. She didn't look at me when I walked in, her hair tied back, her lips close, close together. The TV wasn't even on.

"I want you out," she said.

That's when I saw the bag on the table, the plastic bag I'd hidden in the closet, my stash. It looked frail, guilty, the smoking gun in her case against me. But as far as I was concerned I hadn't committed a crime.

I slammed the door. "You want me out, eh?"

"Yes," she said.

"And how do you plan to manage that?"

She looked up at me, her eyes big, scared. I felt the change, the shift in the climate of the room. I knew what her fear meant. It meant that whatever I did next she wouldn't soon forget.

I grabbed her by the hair and made her stand. The nightie came down to the middle of her thigh, her legs and feet naked, unprepared. I slapped her, aiming for her face but hitting her neck. I slapped her again.

"You don't tell me what to do," I said. "I tell you."

She twisted free, her hair a tangle, her cotton nightie bunched around her breasts.

"You can drink all you want," she said. She tugged down her nightie. Her hands shook. "My dad drank. But this other stuff makes you crazy. It'd make anyone crazy."

She tried to run to the kitchen, but I caught her. *Get out,* she yelled, and I covered her mouth. I felt my power, her more fragile body against mine, the flowery smell of her hair, and I sensed weakness. I held her arms to her sides and waddled with her, Frankenstein-like, to the bedroom. I pushed her onto the bed and held her there.

"I tell *you* what to do," I said. I took my belt off, folded it in half. "I tell *you.*"

The baby cried, and I didn't care. Sally barely acknowledged the beating, and I didn't hesitate. Her blood dotted the sheets, and I didn't stop.

Sally and Josh were gone the next morning, along with the overnight bag, all their clothes, the Pinto. A note sat on the kitchen table. *Everything left here is yours. Everything else is mine.*

* * *

I come out of my house, lock the door behind me. It's dusk, and the grackles make a huge racket in the trees. The Bellinghams—Harv, Jude and the kids—eat barbecue in their back yard like they do every week. Football's started, but it's not cold enough to force them inside. The freeway hums in the distance. I let the screen door slam shut.

I packed my duffel bag with all I need for the trip, and I toss it in the passenger's side of the Grand Torino. Two hundred twenty thousand miles and it's never broken down on me. Let's hope it's got one more in it. I climb in, find the key, start her up. I don't light a cigarette until I hit the interstate.

"A musician," Von said. "Josh tours the country with some band. I forget the name." Forget the name? How could he forget the name?

"Is he singing?" I asked.

"How should I know?" Von said.

I'll tell Josh he comes from a long line of singers, that it's part of his ancestry. I can at least give him that.

I crack the window, let the night suck out my cigarette smoke. The freeway rolls on in front of me, pulled from nothingness by my headlights. I feel drowsy. The pills are in the glove compartment, but I don't want to take one yet. I've got to drive until sunrise. I may not need one at all.

I hit the radio, "Stairway to Heaven," Jesus talk, Clapton, "Rock 'n' Roll Heart." I have to laugh. A rock 'n' roll heart, like that's some special feat. Having a rock 'n' roll heart is the easiest thing in the world. Try getting rid of a rock 'n' roll heart.

Village People

I lean against the backstage door, feel the warmth of it on my shoulders. I've done it. I've walked out on the band. The golden light of the afternoon spills over me. The storefronts across the street look hot and blurry. Cars cruise by along Main Street. The world keeps spinning, and I'm at the center of it, wondering where to jump back on. Or if.

I feel the urge to run, to get as far away as possible, so I make a break for the path, cutting through the overgrowth. I don't know where I'm going, only that I have to get away from the club. I don't want to apologize or be apologized to. I don't want to talk or argue or fistfight it out. I want to get lost in the world and worry about it later.

I've always had a knack for hiding. As a kid, I could hang out indefinitely in clumps of trees or vacant storage rooms or random patches of anything. I told Celia I didn't understand why anyone on the run ever got caught. "It's so easy," I said. "You just stay in your hiding place." "You gotta come out sometime," Celia said. "No, you don't," I said.

Off Main Street, cars turn in and out of parking lots. Superstores extend in both directions. Home Makeover, Office Plus, Dart Mart.

Dart Mart.

My mom used to take me there, at 7:45 on Sunday mornings,

arriving before the doors opened. She scoured the Dart Mart sales ads from the morning paper against the steering wheel.

"Can I look at the toys?" I asked.

"You can look when we get inside, hon," she said.

I was always allowed to bring home one toy. I knew not to pick the fifty-dollar catcher's mitt, or a bike to replace the one I'd just gotten. I could get a Hot Wheels car or some other little thing with no resistance. That was the greatest gift she could've given me, letting me walk up those wide aisles and decide for myself what I wanted. I looked forward to it every week.

When I turned eight I didn't want toys anymore, I wanted records. For my weekly Dart Mart score I could have any single from the American Top Forty, which were lined up one-through-forty at the head of the music section. I had many singles—Styx's "Renegade," Stevie Wonder's "Sir Duke," "The Gambler" by Kenny Rogers—but by the time I got up the nerve to ask for an album, only one artist interested me.

"The Village People?" my mom said, her eyebrows moving down her forehead. "Honey, are you sure you want the Village People?"

Was I sure? What was there not to be sure about? The Village People were everything an eight-year-old boy could want in a pop act, strong, confident men from somewhere far-out, each dressed as an American archetype: the construction worker, the policeman, the army private, the navy midshipman, and Felipe Rose, the American Indian. They sang songs young boys could relate to, "Macho Man," "In the Navy," "Y.M.C.A." Sure, they were gay, but I didn't care about that. I simply felt—in the same way I would later feel about Kiss, Van Halen, and REM—that the Village People kicked some majorly serious ass.

The automatic doors swing open, and I'm engulfed by Dart Mart smell, popcorn, hot dog, with the slightest tinge of plastic. Every Dart Mart has the same smell, the same feel, the same layout. To the right sits the cafeteria, popcorn popper filled to the brim. The cash registers, manned by red-shirted employees, are to the left. The main aisle cuts up the middle. The red and white decor makes me feel like my eyes are being held open by an unseen force. The experience is equal parts dull and refreshing.

I grab a cart and push it up the main aisle. I glide past the racks of women's clothing. Socks, bras, underwear. Giant posters hang from the ceiling, pictures of models dressed as the latest take on the rock 'n' roll kid. Flannel shirts, backward baseball caps, black jeans. Despite the fact that the kids are bent and crouched in positions that must hurt, each has a perfect smile on his face. How fake smiles and weird poses help sell clothes I'll never know, but why else would they do it? If it didn't make money, it wouldn't be here.

In the electronics section, a dozen or so TVs are tuned to the same channel, a movie called *Charade*. Sixties Technicolor, a crowded nightclub, black suits and evening dresses. Cary Grant passes an orange from his neck to Audrey Hepburn's, a game that involves not using your hands. They struggle close to each other, looking both happy and busy, their chins and chests and shoulders trying to keep the orange from falling. Suddenly they stop, and twelve Audreys stare into twelve Carys' eyes. You know she's in love. A pause in the action, a dreamy stare. TV Love. As simple as that.

I had designs on Celia from the first time I saw her at the Green Mansion, a house owned by a group of musicians. She sat on the front porch, blond, barefoot, miniskirted, sipping beer from a plastic cup. She caught me staring at her and came over. "Need a drink?" she asked.

"I'm done for tonight," I said, surprised by her approach, this warm breeze out of nowhere easing its way over to me. "I'm already groggy. I should probably go."

"You can't go," she said. "Who would I talk to?"

Her smile proved she had yet to test the limits of her charm on me.

"Who are you?" I asked.

"Celia," she said. "And you?"

"Josh," I said. "Some still call me Hote."

"Hote," she said. "I like Hote, but I think I'll call you Josh."

"I'd prefer you call me Josh." She laughed a little, more of an audible smile. We'd just met, but somehow I felt like I already knew her. I wouldn't have been surprised if we'd played together as children, at a park or the zoo, sharing a jungle gym while our mothers watched on. I felt the return of a friend lost so long ago I'd forgotten her existence, but not the happiness our time together had brought me.

"So, Josh," she said. "It's time for a refill. Care to join me?"

"I can't," I said. "I've had one too many already. I better go before I embarrass myself."

"Oh," she said. Her golden bangs lay against her forehead. She admitted later she thought I was blowing her off. "Guess I'll see you around."

"Do you want to come with?" I asked, grabbing her wrist as she eased by.

She sat in the passenger seat of my pickup. We drove up University Avenue, the street lamps shining in on us at intervals, each one a little rotating sun. The excitement of having her in my truck shocked me into something close to sobriety, but she sat too far over in the seat, as far away as possible. "Why are you over there?" I asked.

She rolled her eyes. "I shouldn't have come with you."

"Why not?"

"You're getting all the wrong ideas."

"What ideas?" I asked, but I knew what she meant.

She looked out the window, her arms crossed.

"Listen," I said. "I promise to keep my distance if you promise not to worry about it." I reached over, touched her hair. "Please don't worry about it."

She turned towards me. "That's a lot of trust for the first night," she said. "Isn't it a bit early for that kind of trust?"

"It's never too early," I said.

She took a deep breath, uncrossed her arms. She edged closer to me. "So, what are you studying?" she asked.

"I'm not," I said.

"Really?" she said.

"I majored in English right out of high school, but I dropped out a couple years ago."

"I'm English, too," she said. "Are you going back?"

"I don't know," I said. "I'd like to . . . There's this band I'm in that's doing pretty well. I don't think I'll have time for it."

"But you've got to go back," she said. "You've got too much going for you not to go back."

I looked at her, incredulous. "You just met me."

"I know," she said, "but I sense things about people. I sense things about you."

"What do you sense about me?"

She looked straight ahead, her eyes sparkling in the streetlight. "I sense I can trust you," she said.

We parked at the top of South Mountain. The lights of Phoenix spread out before us like the landing space in *Close Encounters of the Third Kind*. We were atop the world looking down, watching it go on without us. Celia sat on the tailgate of my pickup, and I kissed her.

"Remember," she said. "You promised this wouldn't go too far."

"I know. I won't let it go too far."

"I want us to wait."

"I wanna wait, too."

"No, you don't," she said, smiling.

"You're right," I said, "but I'll try—I mean, I can—"

"You can and you will."

* * *

I glide my cart by the camping gear. Sleeping bags, canteens. Celia always tried to get me to go camping. She made me take trips with her to outdoor supply stores, pointed out new gadgets, but I was too into Fun Yung Moon to pay attention. Touring, new songs, record contracts, it all seemed too important to be off the grid for so long.

Miniature tents, army green and maroon, the perfect size for Barbie and G.I. Joe, line the aisle, small versions of the full-sized tents. I unzip the front door of one of them and stick my hand in. It's cozy in there, tranquil. It makes me want to crawl in and disappear. The vinyl of the tent makes a nice *zip zip zip* sound between my fingers.

I could do it, you know.

I could buy some camping gear right here today and drop out of sight. It would give me a chance to take a break, maybe make it out to the coast. I wouldn't have to worry about Celia. She thinks I'm on the road, and the band . . .

I scan the camping gear. I wouldn't need a tent. It would call too much attention to itself. All I'd need is a sleeping bag. I could sleep under the stars, maybe under some trees if the weather gets bad.

I pick up one of the sleeping bags, which come in cardboard boxes. There's a picture of a family on the outside, a father, mother, two children, all roasting marshmallows. How many people actually come from this nuclear family anymore? Hardly anyone, but the ideal lingers on. Just like the band. Radio play, touring the country, people cheering, what more could a musician ask for?

We have a tour to finish, not to mention a gig tonight. I'd be stranding them, ditching them in the middle of a job. No one in Fun Yung Moon has ventured into this territory, and I know why. Because there's no going back. The others—Gad, Forrest, Verge—might be able to forgive me someday, but they'd never trust me again.

I look at the cardboard box, feel the lightness of the sleeping bag inside. But what do *I* want? There's everybody else—Celia, the band, everything the world expects of me—and then there's me. Who exactly do I hurt when I live the life I want to live? I know who I hurt when I don't. I drop the box into the cart.

Fuck Gad. Fuck him to high heaven. Let him scramble a bit for the grief he's caused me. Fife's a guitar player; he could take over on bass for the rest of the tour. He sat in for Verge one night when Verge drank too much cough medicine and couldn't make it to the stage. Fife already knows most of the songs, and he's got my bass rig to play on. He'll be fine. If they can't figure that out, that's their problem.

Air mattresses!

They're thinner than the ones I remember, flat like a bath mat, not puffy like the kind around the swimming pool where I grew up. These expand into sleek, even pads. Perfect for camping. I drop one into the cart.

What else do I need? A lantern? Matches? A little pillow? No. I want to travel light.

I could use a change of clothes. My bag's back at the hotel, but it's too much to carry. I don't care about that stuff anyway. Clothes, books, all things replaceable.

I push my cart to the men's clothes section. Mannequins wear decaled T-shirts—"Amazing Me," "I'm with Stupid." Packaged socks hang from hooks on the wall. Swim trunks dangle from a circular rack, thin, billowy material, the kind that dries fast.

The beach can't be far from here. I didn't see it on the way down, but I could find it if I had to. How long has it been? Last New Year's Eve, Celia dropped her Christmas bonus on a hotel room at Rocky Point, but it was too cold to get in the water. Our San Diego honeymoon was years ago. Nowhere do I feel more removed than at the beach. The weather's warm enough, too.

I flip through the swim trunks. What size am I these days? I know I've put on weight since the band, but I've been afraid to find out how much. I twist backwards and turn up the back of my pants. "38." I don't feel like a thirty-eight. I find the thirty-eight section and flip through them. There's only one non-orange pair, emerald green, baggy in the crotch but not hanging down to the knees. I hold them up to the light. They seem too big, but they'll work. I toss them into the cart.

What else will I need? Food.

I push my cart to the food section. Brightly colored packages line the shelves. Ruffles, Frito's, Little Debbies. Since the band got signed, I've gotten used to a higher standard of fare. I remember when Glen took me to that expensive place in L.A., the name so foreign I couldn't even pronounce it. We ordered dishes that looked like works of art, had drinks that came in little wooden boxes. Glen got a kick out of having someone to impress. "The flavor of the wood seeps into the wine," Glen explained. He took a drink from his box. "They've been doing it for centuries in Asia."

I drank from my box. It tasted sharp, like white wine, but also with a wood flavor. I felt refined, eating exotic food, tasting what I was supposed to taste. "This is great," I said. "Why haven't they started doing this all over? I could see kids using these at keggers."

Glen laughed. "That's what I love about you, Hote. You think things *could* happen the way they *should*."

"What's that supposed to mean?" I said. "You think I'm naive?"

Glen raised his box in a toast. "You're exactly how you should be, Hote. You're hopeful. May you always be so hopeful."

I try to avoid pre-packaged food, but I go weak when I see the bags of Chips Ahoy cookies. How many Chips Ahoys I ate when I was a kid I don't know, but there may not be numbers that go that high. Something about the package calls to me. I grab it and set it in the cart.

The dozen or so checkout counters are mostly untended, but a girl stands behind one at the far end. She's young, very young, with pigtails that stick straight out from her head like Pippy Longstocking. This look never would've flown at a Dart Mart when I was growing up, but times change. Rock 'n' roll has infiltrated everything.

"Going camping?" she says when I put my sleeping bag on the counter. Her red Dart Mart polo is tied in a knot at her belly, and her black miniskirt barely covers the essentials.

"That's not what I'd call it."

"What would you call it?"

"Taking a little break," I say. I set the Chips Ahoys on the counter.

"I see you have all the necessities."

"Am I forgetting anything?"

"Not really," she says. "It's all in what you can handle. Are you going far?"

"Not tonight."

"Well, then I'd say you're stocked up. You might want to grab a bottle of water." She points to a display of gallon jugs at the head of the checkout lane. I completely forgot about water. I grab one and set it on the counter.

She twists the bottle towards her and scans it. The red scramble of the scanner reflects up and causes a nice shimmer in her eyes. She bends way over and drops the bottle into the cart, not caring that anyone coming from the other way could see right up her skirt.

"How'd you get your hair to do that?" I ask.

"Mm?" she says. She's having trouble getting the air mattress to scan.

"I asked how you got your hair like that."

"Easy," she says. She tosses the mattress into the cart. "Copper wire and hair spray."

"It looks great," I say.

"It totally pisses my boss off," she says, "which is all I care about."

"Don't like your job?" I ask.

She scans the Chips Ahoys and drops them, with a crunch, into the baby seat of the cart. "It's necessary if I ever want to get out of here."

"Where do you want to go?"

"Out of here," she says, punching numbers into the register.

Glen

The goals for a signed band are simple. Keep in the game, stay together, write songs, tour. Do all the things that keep the wheel greased for all of us. You have to milk that initial rush for all it's worth; it's the only one you get, and they'll all be shocked at how difficult it is to get the ball rolling again once it stops. They won't understand. "Why does everything get reflected off our first hit?" Because that's the way it is. That's the game you signed up for. As soon as you start losing members, or singing songs written by other people, or taking a year off to raise a kid, you're in danger of looking like the honeymoon's over. Has it been over for a while already? Of course it has, but the perception is far more important than that. We're knee-deep in a game of perception. Reality has to compromise to make room for it.

Now, do I go around thumping my chest about this to Fun Yung Moon? No. Absolutely no. "Never tell a client the truth," Balstein said when he signed me on to his management company ten years ago. I was a gullible kid from Nebraska who loved Springsteen; I would've worked in the music business for free. "You take the truth, combine it with a good dose of pragmatism, add a dash of greed, cook until done, and serve it to the band with a side of compliments about their good looks and positive contribution to society. Do that, and charge twenty percent of gross, and you'll never have a problem."

I've talked many a performer down from the ledge, where one false move would send them plummeting head first into the straight world. I haven't lost one yet. By the time I'm done with them, they always see it my way.

My best work was Bergot. You know him. He had that hit in the eighties, "What You Want," that was so generic everyone thought it was about them. What most people don't know is Bergot was ready to give it all up. He got caught up in some religious books, thought he wanted to move to Tibet and become a monk. Balstein sent me to New York in his place. "He likes you," Balstein said. "If I go, I'll probably kill him."

I met him at his loft. This wasn't the first of Bergot's threats to throw it all away, but he was serious this time. All of his furniture was grouped in the middle of the room, ready to be picked up. He'd already sold his guitars, and the grand piano the record company'd bought him had disappeared. The room was hot, the windows shut and bolted, the power already turned off. He was taking nothing but a backpack. "You can burn whatever's left," he said.

"Bergie," I said. "Your fans love you. Your label loves you. What's the problem?" The guy'd just finished a tour of Japan that brought in more money than God could've made.

"No problem," he said. He stuffed his backpack with clothes, more than it could fit. "It's my career, right?"

"Of course."

"Then I'm choosing to end it," he said, smiling at me. You could see the radiance that sold all those people on him in the first place. His eyes were like two corners of a long triangle formed with his Adam's apple. The dark hair that was so famously done up in the "What You Want" video hung in his face. He pushed it behind his ears as he packed.

"If that's what you want, then that's what Balstein and I and everyone else want for you," I lied. "We just have to make sure it's really what you want."

"Did you know that Bhuddist monks have no money?" he said. He flipped his hair out of his eyes. "They roam the streets all day. They beg for their dinner. They sleep under a tree or next to a river or in an alley. They don't care about any of this."

"That's amazing," I said. "But do they have what you have?"

He smiled, but the smile had bite. "What exactly do I have?"

"A great career, for one. Fans who'd do anything for you. Friends, money. Hell, Bergie, what don't you have?"

That made him laugh. He looked at me, wondering if I knew how full of shit I was, and went back to packing.

"Where'd the piano go?" I asked.

"I gave it to the neighbors."

"*Gave* it to them?"

"Two teenagers," he said. "They're trying to put a band together. I figured they'd put it to good use."

"Do you know how much it's worth?"

"Fuck it, Glen," he said.

Selflessness, a desire to dedicate himself to goodness and rightness, a blatant disregard for the money machine we'd spent years perfecting, this guy had to be stopped and I had to stop him.

"What about Marcus?" I said.

That made him hesitate. He put down the shirt he was trying to cram into his bag. "What about him?"

He'd met Marcus on his last video shoot. A dancer. Berg insisted Marcus come on the tour of Japan, and we were only too happy to accommodate him. If it kept his fits in check, we were all for it. "How does he feel about this?" I said.

"We live different lives," Berg said. He resumed his stuffing. "You can't expect creative people to just drop everything to be together."

"Is he in town?"

"How would I know? He doesn't feel the need to tell me anything."

Two sofas were face-to-face, and I had to hop over the back of one to sit down. "That's a shame," I said. "He made you happy. I could tell."

To my surprise, Berg started crying. Now, I'm not crazy about people crying in front of me, but a rock star crying in front of me is intolerable. We work like hell to make these guys happy, but you try it. Nothing short of world domination works. Berg's face went from thoughtful to shriveled to crushed. The tears dripped from his chin onto the hard wood floor.

"Bergie," I said. I climbed back over the couch and went to him. "Things happen. People get mad, then they get weird, and sometimes, somewhere in there, love happens. That's about the best we can hope for." I put my hand on his shoulder. He wouldn't look up. "Or so I've heard."

He laughed a little. My love life, which amounts to big tips left at the massage parlor on Friday afternoons—and sometimes on Tuesday nights—is common fodder for everyone. Fine. Let them have their laugh. I'm not the one balling my eyes out over a dancer who's probably screwed half the New York Mets.

"You don't know the half of it," Berg said.

"But how's running away going to help anything?" I said. "You're an artist. You've got to channel it, turn it into something people want."

"No," he yelled. He picked up his backpack and threw it against the wall. His clothes went everywhere. Tracks of tears slanted down from his eyes. "I write songs, I record them, people love them or hate them. It's like an auction of my soul, and I'm over it. My feelings aren't for everyone else anymore. I'm not selling them to the highest bidder or putting them on parade or giving them away for free. From now on, my feelings are *mine*."

That was my window. I could smell it coming, the moment when his need and my need and the heat in the room would pop a mushroom that would save us all. "That's the most un-monk-like thing I've ever heard," I said.

He looked at me with venom in his eyes.

"Bergie," I said. "You have something that very few people have in this world. You have a gift. You travel to the edges of the emotional landscape and you come back with these crystals of pathos, these songs of beautiful pain, and you deliver them to the world, and guess what? *The world is better for it.* The world heals because of what you do. You're not a monk. A monk would be the biggest waste of you imaginable. You're a medicine man, Bergie. A shaman. Do you know how rare that is?"

Berg just stood there, hands in his pockets, hair drooping into his face. By his posture and the way my words sounded in the room, I could tell I'd hit home. "Don't you think that's a bit lofty?" he said. "I mean, it's pop music."

"Horse shit," I said. "That's horse shit, and you know it. You're the one who plays songs while twenty thousand people sing along. You're the one who signs autographs for four hours every time you have an in-store. You're the one who gets ten-page letters from fans who go on and on about how much your music means to them. Can you possibly tell me that it doesn't matter because it's 'pop music'? That it's some kind of lucky mistake and all the lives that have changed because of it don't amount to squat? It touches people, Berg. That's the only proof there is of anything."

The room was quiet, and Berg looked down. The look reminded me of a moment in one of his videos, "Promised Land," a close-up of him as he sings the song, the words not muttered so much as falling out of his mouth. I remember the filming of that segment, one of the last shots of the night. Berg was tired and bored, doing whatever the director told him, waiting for it all to be over so he could go home. Somehow in the video he doesn't look bored at all. He looks pensive, solemn, even angelic. The magic of film, I guess, or maybe the magic of Berg. Who cares which.

Berg glanced around, at the thrown bag, the clothes everywhere, the furniture sucked together like magnets in the center of the room. "I'm moving," he said. "I can't do New York anymore."

"Fine," I said. "Where do you want to go?"

He thought for a second. "You're from Nebraska. How'd you like it?"

"Put it this way," I said. "You move to Nebraska, you won't have to worry about me dropping by."

* * *

Here's what I'll tell Hote when he calls—and he'd better call. Being a rock star has nothing to do with talent. If it just took talent, there'd be more rock stars than managers and lawyers and accountants combined. So what makes a rock star? What's the one trait Dylan and Bono and Lou Reed all have that the rest of us don't have a clue about? Here it is. Rock stars can accept the love of millions of people they don't know. That's it. That's all it takes. Sound easy? Most of us can't do it. That much love would turn us into babbling idiots. Gad can accept that love. So can Verge. Hote had better learn how, because this train rolls with or without him, and Fun Yung Moon beats the hell out of working at Kinko's for the rest of your life.

And what if he does quit? What if the kid throws away everything and bails on his band? Things'll be fine for a while. He'll take a vacation, go to Cabo or Tahiti, get caught up in the possibilities of a laid back life. Then, he'll come home with a new perspective, an even tan, and try a side project or two. When those fail, he'll putter around the house, get worked up about things like the evening news, and his wife will get sick of having him around. That's when he'll call me, and I'll say, "Hote? Sorry. I don't know anyone by that name."

Removal/Retrieval

I pick up the receiver of the pay phone outside Dart Mart. My cart's lodged in a sidewalk crack to keep it from rolling away. The sun elongates the shadows of trees. Evening's coming. Celia should be home from work by now.

I dial my home. Cars seem to slow as they ease by. People look over. "I'm just a guy on a pay phone," I want to say. I feel exposed, vulnerable, like someone might approach me at any minute, put a hand on my shoulder and say, "Fun's over, Hote. Time to come with us." The sky seems too close overhead. I crave cover.

Celia isn't answering. The thought that she could be gone for good sends a chill over me. I'd never see her again, never get a chance to talk it out. I hang up the phone and quickly dial her cell. It rings once. "This is Celia," she says.

My throat tightens. Her presence, the mere presence of her voice, is a sign of hope.

"Josh?"

"Yeah."

"It is you. Listen, we have to talk."

"Great."

"You hung up before I could explain."

"What's there to explain?" I say. "You jumped the fence, Celia. What more needs to be said?"

I hear her sigh. She's struggling to keep her cool, to let me have my moment. "I just wanted you to know—" She pauses. "It was one night, Josh. That's it. One night. I've never seen him again, and I never will."

Her words bring relief—I'm glad it's not serious—but for some reason I say, "Is that supposed to make a difference?"

"Would anything make a difference?" she says.

A good question. "I don't know," I say. "I know I resent being in this position. I resent you putting me in this position."

In the parking lot an attendant, pushing a long line of carts, jerks the whole line, and the wheels grind against the pavement.

"Where are you?" she says.

"I'm out in the world, Celia," I say, "and you know what? I like it out here. I'm not ready to come home yet. You'll hear from me when I am." And I hang up the phone.

My wedding ring is still on my finger. That ring gave my days shape, created walls that became the house for my soul. Not anymore. I slide my ring off, throw it as hard as I can towards the back of Dart Mart.

My life, vanished. For a brief moment, I'm exhilarated. All that's left are me, and Dart Mart, these manicured lawns and the rest of these superstores. What else could I possibly need? Everything vital's been missing for years now—the passion, the urgency. Hell. Even Digs Ven is dead.

Digs, the booted lead guitarist and chief songwriter of the Prior Angels, the reason that band went from Tempe bars to headlining stadiums across the country. It'll be three years this December since he did himself in, shot himself, succeeded in his third try at suicide. Kurt Cobain came to the same conclusion months later, and had Digs waited he surely would've been lumped into a copycat category. Digs never copied anyone. His guitar tone was loud—like Cobain's and a million others—but also clean, like someone had broken into the Beach Boys' practice room and turned their amps up when they weren't looking. His songs—crushingly sweet melodies that bring back the best of fifties pop—share with Cobain's only a self-deprecating lyrical bent. And his stage presence. Possessed from the first note, Digs jumped and kicked, wielding his guitar like it was a wild animal he desperately wanted to get rid of. Onstage, as a musician and songwriter, as a sardonic wit, Digs personified the rock 'n' roll dream. He was my hero.

I remember the last time I saw him, after a gig at Richmond's with his new band, Actual Size. Fun Yung Moon had started to get attention from Amythyst Records, and Gad was cultivating the idea of throwing Lance out of the band. Digs had been through it all with the Prior Angels, and I wanted his take, or maybe I just wanted to talk to him. I waited for him by a telephone pole just outside the stage door.

He came out an hour after the show, his cowboy hat shadowing his half-moon face. He dug into his jean-jacket pocket and removed a pack of cigarettes, sticking one between his lips. He lit it as he walked by.

"I wanted to tell you you were right," I said.

"Huh?" he said. I'd startled him, and he swayed backwards, his lanky frame drifting in an attempt to see me. He was drunk. He took the cigarette from his mouth and squinted through his bangs, wondering where he knew me from, or if he knew me at all. I didn't think he'd recognize me; rumor had it his eyes were failing. "Right about what?"

"About lead singers being the bane of your existence."

We bought a twelve-pack—"It's after-hours," I said as we pulled into the Circle K parking lot. Digs held up his gig money. "If you're willing to drop a twenty on a twelve-pack, it's never after-hours."—and we drank it together on top of 'A' Mountain. Phoenix stretched out before us. The few skyscrapers poked up like unused matches in an old book. The suburbs rolled out in all directions, their light radiating up to the sky. Even Digs could see it.

"That's the best thing about this god forsaken place," Digs said, pointing to the view. He took a tug of his longneck. "It sure as hell ain't the weather. Good Christ! If I have to spend another summer here I'm gonna chop my head off."

"Or Joel's," I said. On the way up the mountain we'd taken turns plotting the deaths of our respective lead singers. Decapitation came up early and often. Most of the twelve-pack was gone.

"I flattened him once at Richmond's," Digs said.

"Really?"

"He came in—this is after all the lawyer bullshit—and wanted to patch things up. I decked him right there, once in the jaw, and he went down."

"I wish I had the guts to do that," I said. "Gad's got one coming."

"So, what's up with Gad, anyway?" Digs asked.

"Oh, the usual," I said. "He makes every decision, and the rest of us just have to deal with it. He wants to throw Lance out of the band." I took a tug of my beer. "Did you know he won't even consider anyone else's songs? I quit writing."

"Listen," Digs said. He sat up on his rock—these outcroppings of sandstone—and looked at me. "If you're gonna stay with this band you need to understand two things. Thing one." He held up an index finger. "This guy is not your friend."

"No problem there," I said.

"Good," he said. "Thing two. Even though this guy's not your friend, you still need him."

"What?" I said. I sat up on my rock. "Fuck that. I don't need Gad."

"Yes," Digs said. He waved his finger in the air. "You need him."

"Bullshit," I said. "You ditched Joel, and you got into a new band right away."

"Yeah," he said, "but the Angels—" Digs smiled, the Phoenix light reflecting off his eyes. "The Angels had magic. I can't explain it. No one can, but we all knew it. You just know. No matter what I do from here on out, the Angels were where my magic happened. Nothing's gonna change that."

I'd seen part of Actual Size's set. They were good, not great. It was a little unsettling to see Digs onstage with anyone else. He didn't quite fit in, this tall, angular rock star up there with mere mortals. Still, I said, "That's way premature. Some of your new songs are great. You guys just need some time to gel."

"Time to gel," Digs said, smiling. His cigarette pack lay on the rock next to him, and he slid one out. "Sounds like what people say when they're trying to be nice."

"I'm not trying to be nice," I lied. I stood up, frustrated. I launched my empty beer bottle down the mountain. We both listened to it shatter. "You're Digs Ven, for Christ's sake, the best songwriter in town. If anybody can, you can."

"It doesn't work like that," Digs said. He lit his cigarette, flicked the match away. Smoke eased out his nose. "Your soul is your soul, Hote. I left mine onstage with the Angels. It sounds like yours is tangled up with this Gad character."

"No way," I said. "I'm not answering to Gad for the rest of my life. I'd quit tomorrow before I'd let that happen."

"Well," he said. "Don't do anything drastic until after you get signed. If you don't think you can hang with it, at least get paid first."

"Get paid?" I said. "Is that what this is all about? I thought we played music because we didn't care about money."

Digs finished his beer with a backward tilt of his head. He pushed himself off the rock. "You can ride that train as long as you want," he said. He launched his empty down the mountain. *Shatter.* "Just make sure the bar's well-stocked."

* * *

Rush hour makes Main Street lopsided. All the traffic heads in one direction, south from Los Angeles towards the suburbs. The sun angles between two business signs. I need a place to sleep.

I ease my cart over to the stand of trees between Dart Mart and the Equinox. I've never done anything like this before, and I feel the pressure of being a trespasser. Someone could shoot me right now and probably get off scot-free.

The trees slant outward, the limbs growing unchecked over the lot. I peek inside and find a little clearing, limbs pushed aside or removed, leaves raked away.

Through the other side, the band's bus is parked behind the club, its nose angled for a quick escape tonight. The sight of it—its large, square presence, the chrome and navy exterior—makes their departure seem inevitable. It's happening. That bus is leaving for Fresno tonight, with or without me.

I grab the bag of Chips Ahoy, the water, and pull up a seat on the ground. Nothing stirs in the parking lot or by the club. There's no search party out looking for me. At least twenty minutes goes by and nothing happens. Half the bag of Chips Ahoy disappears.

I have a few books on board the bus, something to do until the sun goes down. The band and crew are back at the hotel, getting ready or checking out or stealing a last moment of solitude. I could grab a book and be gone before anyone sees me. If I want to do it, now's the time.

I shuffle through the trees into the parking lot. I try to go slow— I don't want to look like a thief—but it takes too long so I hustle the last bit to the bus door.

Inside, the bus glows with the red color of the drawn shades. The air's muggy. The generator's been turned off, no air conditioning. Someone's left a full bag of laundry on one of the couches.

I'm amazed at how boring it feels in here. Tour buses are supposed to be palaces of rock 'n' roll debauchery, drugs, booze, chicks everywhere. Instead, ours feels almost domestic. The little kitchen—sink, refrigerator, microwave—could be the same in any travel trailer. The couches are perfectly comfortable for lounging or watching TV. A stack of CDs sits on the table under the stereo, just like a teenager's bedroom.

I go to the sleeping area and pull back the curtain of my bunk. Books are wedged between the mattress and the wall: a Vonnegut collection, *Ulysses*, and *The Hamer Anthology of English Literature*, the latter a leftover from the semester I went back to school with Celia. I grab it and flip through it, the pages thin like onionskin. The spine breaks naturally at the page with a poem by John Donne called "The Good-Morrow." Notes are scribbled in the margins, penciled hearts and arrows. "Hey, you," one note says, an attempt to get Celia's attention during class. "Yes, you," the next one says. "I love you." Despite what's happened, this book is priceless, a prime slice of my life. I can't believe I almost let it go.

I remember lying on her mattress with her, holding the book above us, reading the poem out loud to each other. The line "One little room an everywhere" always made us smile. We were fusing, Celia and me, like molecules forming a new element. I felt it in the way she read the poem, saw it in her eyes. Our marriage was an attempt to consummate that fusion.

I look up when I hear the latch of the bus door. My head spins with a million possibilities, none of them good. For a second I think of climbing into my bunk, but there's no time. Here they come. Stand up and take it like a man.

"Hey, Hote."

It's Lookout, the bus driver, and I breathe a little easier. That it's Lookout is both a blessing and a curse, a blessing because he's unlikely to know the events of the day, a curse because Lookout loves company. It will be impossible to get away.

"Hey, Lookout," I say.

Lookout stomps up the stairs, an ear-to-ear grin at the unexpected surprise of finding me here. That grin is his best weapon in his never-ending war to keep people around him. His white muscle shirt clings to his frame, revealing just how skinny he is, and curls of black hair stick to his skull. He carries an empty turquoise bucket.

Where do they get these bus drivers? Sure, they need a trucker's mentality, and they need to be willing to drive all night, but does that disqualify anyone who's halfway sane? Our last driver, Manny, smoked speed at the wheel. The guy before him, "Slow Ride," screwed groupies two at a time until we got complaints from parents and had to fire him. Lookout talks. And talks. And talks. After twenty minutes of non-stop jabbering you start to wonder, doesn't his throat get sore? His jaw tired? The guys in the band avoid him like the plague. No wonder Lookout's wife doesn't mind that he's on the road ten months a year.

"Fancy meeting you here," Lookout says. "Thought you were away doing your thing."

"Nope," I say. "I'm around. What's up?"

"Washing the bus," he says. He lifts the bucket to show me. "The club owner said I can use the spigot out back. Gotta wash this fucker every once in a while or it starts to look like shit."

Lookout's cuss words don't come naturally. They seem a habit he's adopted for road life, something to gain approval from the rest of us. Instead, they sound phony, a wayward Christian too conscious of his sin.

"That's great," I say. I make my move, a slight lowering of my head and a quick step towards the door. "I was just grabbing my book and–"

"You wanna help?" Lookout asks.

For some reason, I hesitate. You have to admire his guts, asking a band member to help him with odd jobs. I wonder if anyone in Soul Asylum or Garth Brooks or Slayer has to put up with this. How many records would Fun Yung Moon have to sell before Lookout gets too intimidated to ask me to help him wash the bus? Five million? Ten?

Lookout swings the bucket, smiling ear-to-ear.

* * *

A compartment underneath houses a garden hose, some soap, and sections of metal tube that screw together to make one long pole. A square mop pops on the end.

"Look at this thing," Lookout says. He swings it in the air, a college cheerleader waving the school flag. "Twelve feet. I keep it with me no matter who I tour with. You wanna try it?"

I take the pole and stare up at the mop head, spongy gold against the blue sky.

"Pretty cool, huh?" Lookout says. "Hold it against the bus. I'll get the bucket ready."

I put the mop head against the bus. I like the way it feels, the inch or two of sponge disappearing as I push it into the panel. This could be fun. Even strokes. Spray it down. Rainbows.

Lookout comes back with an overflowing bucket of soapy water, his arm pulled tight by the weight.

"You mind if I do this part?" I ask, motioning to the mop.

"You can do whatever you want," Lookout says. "I'll do the rims while you do the panels. Let me get the jam box." He disappears into the bus.

I slide the pole down in my hands and dip the mop into the bucket, try not to drip on myself as I angle it back up. I push the mop against the bus, and it gushes soapy water. *Plenty* is the word that pops into my head. Plenty of bus, plenty of tool, plenty of soap, plenty of water, a chore so plentiful it almost does itself. I pull the mop down the side. It takes more muscle than I would've thought, but the streak left behind is clean and perfect. What's the world coming to? Even good, honest work feels decadent.

Lookout comes back with a jam box and a stack of CDs, losing one with a clatter onto the pavement. "What do you wanna listen to? I've got all kinds of stuff—Supertramp, Prior Angels, Lyle Lovett. You like the Angels?"

"Absolutely," I say.

"Angels it is," he says.

The music kicks in, "Of Age Tonight," a Digs song about falling in love with a girl "just past fifteen." It's not the first cut on the record—Lookout must've hit the shuffle button—and it's mellower than the rest, soft, fluttery guitars under Joel's crooning voice. I remember Celia listening to it once just after we'd moved into our new house, a Saturday after too much wine on Friday night. Celia cleaned the living room, her hair tied back in a scarf, wearing a white, loose-fitting blouse I could see through, and old jeans. I accosted her in the living room, made her put down the Pledge and escorted her into the bedroom. The girl looked sexy even dusting furniture. Maybe more so.

Lookout dunks a sponge into the bucket. "It's great you're helpin'," he says. "These things take hours to do by yourself. You like washin' stuff?"

Do I like washing stuff? "Yeah," I say. "I like washing stuff."

"Great," he says. He's found a milk crate somewhere, and he sets it upside-down next to the tires of the bus, squats on it. "It seems like as soon as I clean this fucker it gets dirty again. Can you believe how fast it gets dirty?"

"It's pretty dirty," I say. I dunk the mop head into the bucket.

"Hote?"

"Yeah?"

"Did you know that guy from the Prior Angels who killed himself?"

"Digs?" I say.

"Yeah."

I angle the mop head against the bus. I'm not sure how much I want to share with Lookout about Digs. I pull the mop down the panel. "He was a guy I knew," I say. "We weren't best friends. We had a couple beers together a couple times."

"You know why he did it?"

"I don't know exactly," I say. I dunk the mop into the water. "But he wasn't in the Angels when he killed himself. They threw him out before that."

"Really?" Lookout says. "Why'd they throw him out?"

"They'll tell you it was his drinking," I say. "But I don't think that's the real reason."

"What's the real reason?"

"The real reason is bands drift apart," I say. "After a while it gets too uncomfortable to be in the same room together, and you find a reason to shake someone out. The Angels' excuse was Digs's drinking, but it could've been anything."

"Oh," Lookout says.

"They may not hate each other," I say. "They could still even love each other, but they sure as hell don't like each other anymore."

"Sounds like a marriage," Lookout says.

I stop scrubbing. "Why do you say that?"

"I don't know," he says. "Just that the same thing can happen in a marriage. Your wife spends too much money, or she stays out late or whatever, and it isn't because she wants to do that stuff as much as she wants to . . . you know . . . do it against you."

"I guess I know what you mean," I say, which isn't quite true. I bring the mop head down and dunk it into the water.

"It's not like I don't have opportunities," Lookout says. He's got his rim washing technique down—a quick, half-circle wipe on one side, then switch the sponge to the other hand and do the other side. "Out on the road, girls around all the time, I could do it whenever I wanted, but do I ever take advantage of it?"

"No," I say, not remembering Lookout ever taking advantage of it—but also not remembering him having too many opportunities.

"I never want to because that would be the end of it," he says.

"Not my marriage—I mean, I could get away with it—but the end of what it's supposed to be. It wouldn't mean anything if I just did it whenever the chance came up."

"I agree," I say. "It wouldn't mean anything."

"But it's not the same for her," he says.

"How is it for her?"

He picks up the sponge, wrings it out. The suds are gone, nothing left but murky water. "There's this guy," he says, "our neighbor, Reg. He just got this new RV—a nice RV, I admit it, okay? It's a nice RV. So, I call her yesterday and she answers her cell phone *in his RV*. She doesn't even try to hide it. She tells me, 'I'm just hanging out with Reg in his RV.' I tell her I don't like it, that I don't want her there, that she isn't allowed in Reg's RV. She just laughs."

Divorce her, I want to say. Divorce her right now. Call a lawyer and get the whole thing under way. Being unfaithful's one thing, being cruel's another. "Well," I say. "I guess I don't know what to say, Lookout. I think it's wrong she does that to you."

"That's what I tell her," Lookout says. "I tell her not to embarrass me in front of Reg, to side—to *laugh* with him—against me."

"I don't think she should do that."

"Me, neither," he says. He stands up, picks up his milk crate and sets it down in front of the next rim. The sun shines on the back of his neck, tufts of black hair buzzed to almost nothing. He's going to burn. "But what do you do?"

What do you do? The question of the day. If I were Lookout, I'd know what to do, but I'm not Lookout. I don't know his wife, and I never loved her. I love Celia, and I couldn't listen to anyone tell me how I should handle our marriage. There are no rule books, nothing that says we have to act this way or that. The only rule books are inside of us, our hearts. We have to keep them unbroken.

* * *

It takes an hour, but we finish the bus. I rushed the last bit, not taking the time to work every smudge off, but the bus glistens like new. It's almost gig time, and I'm afraid people will start showing up. I grab my book and tell Lookout I'm going back to the hotel, even though I'm never going to see him again.

"Here," Lookout says. He hands me the Prior Angels CD.

"No," I say. I try to give it back. "You don't need to pay me. I helped because I wanted to."

Lookout holds up his hands. "Take it," he says. "That way I won't feel so bad when I ask you next time."

Betty

Find me people who want to start a punk band. Tell me where they are, and I'll go get them.

And I mean a real punk band, not some MTV fluffer band that grimaces for the camera. Real punk comes from within. It has nothing to do with spitting in the right direction. It doesn't worry about what it looks like or who it offends. No one ever taught me how to be punk. I knew it before it knew me.

All the other cashiers at Dart Mart are Hispanic. They wouldn't get the Descendents. They wouldn't get Negativland. They wouldn't get Einsturzende Neubauten. They paint their nails blue and their eyelids pink. When they stretch, they bend their hands backwards. To play guitar you have to bend your hand the other way, towards the wrist, and if you want to play it low, like the Ramones, you have to bend it far, far up. I learned to play guitar low.

I could tell I was punk the first time I heard the Dead Kennedys at Goo's place that summer I turned fourteen. I'd hang at his apartment all day. He'd be off working, but I liked to be there anyway. I'd lie on the floor of his living room and listen to records. I'd dig through his milk crates. I'd put on his clothes. I'd be waiting for him when he came home. "Do you think we'll get married some day?" I asked him once after sex. That made him laugh.

Chelsea says they miss me at school. She says Kyle won't shut up about how I'm not going to college, about teen pregnancy and welfare queens. I told her Kyle will cheat his way through State, marry the first girl he sleeps with, and work the same lame job every day for the rest of his life. Kyle wouldn't know guts if it came gushing at him out of a pony keg.

At work, I wear my skirts short. I wear socks pulled up to the knee, combat boots. There's no end to the crew manager's suggestions, the glances. It's shock I'm after, and it's shock I get. That's part of the deal. I'll only work this job if I can offend a few people along the way.

The store's slow today. Even Alejandro quit pretending to stock. I rely on the customers to entertain me. Like the camper, his coyness, the way he tried to flirt. Those are the people I like, the ones with something cooking just beneath the surface. Signs of life.

If five o'clock ever gets here, Stuart and I will rock the house, his house, where his drums are, the peach sparkle Gretsch kit his folks bought him for Christmas. Cute kid. Twelve years old and completely in love with me. I'm trying to save him from those hippies at Revolution Music—they teach him nothing but Beatles songs and paradiddles—but his parents won't let him quit. They're afraid his drums are gonna wind up in the closet like every other hobby he's tried. "But we won't let that happen, will we, Stu?" I said. He split his face smiling when I said that.

The clock ticks above Customer Service. Four forty-one, the second hand never quite stopping.

Goo.

What a number he did on me two summers ago, Green Day on the radio, me ready to start high school. I met him at an all-ages show at the V.F.W.—they let kids play shows there during the summer, and that night some Pearl Jam wannabe band gave it their all onstage. Goo sat in a booth by himself. His green mohawk added four inches to his height. I'm a sucker for a mohawk, and he was sexy, skateboard skinny, wearing black from head to toe. I ditched Chelsea right away and sauntered over, slid into the booth seat across from him.

"Who are you, and what are you doing here?" I asked. He looked bored but also within his element, like he'd cultivated boredom into a style all his own.

He crunched ice from his cup. "This is the only show in town, right?" he said. "I didn't feel like driving all the way to L.A."

I loved the veins in his hands, his voice, his 'R's curling around his lips. He gave me warm fuzzies in places I reserved solely for Billie Joe Armstrong. "If I had a car I'd go to L.A. all the time," I said.

He leaned over the table and touched my hand. I felt the calluses on his palms. "Sweetheart," he said. He smiled, revealing a gap at the back of his mouth, a missing tooth. "You sure you're old enough to go to shows in L.A.?" That smile sealed the deal.

He drove me back to his apartment, an unfurnished studio his parents rented for him to keep him out of the house. I learned all about him. His name was Goo, or at least that's what he went by. He was seventeen, almost eighteen. He dropped out of high school because he wanted to see the world and he probably would've failed out anyway. He worked construction; the money was great, and it would get him out of Orange County the quickest. He wanted to move to San Francisco. That's where the Dead Kennedys are from, and that was all he needed to know. By his estimation, he'd be there by fall. I got my virginity out of the way, and we spent the rest of the summer together.

* * *

Five o'clock, and I'm in my car in thirty seconds. A blue Ford Festiva, the booty from my sixteenth birthday. It's not the best car in the world—I mean, it's no Dodge Dart—but I love it anyway. I plastered it with bumper stickers—Minutemen, Buzzcocks, Flaming Lips. The hatchback is just the right size for a Marshall half stack I've got my eye on. A few more months as Dart Mart's bad-girl checkout attendant and it's all mine.

Stuart will be waiting for me at his house. I told him I'd be there, in tune, ready to rock, at five fifteen. The kid's a natural on the drums. He already knows how to play really fast. Now all he has to do is show up to practice and keep his nose out of drugs. "I'll try," he said, "but it's hard for a happenin' dude like me." That made both of us laugh.

I bounce my Festiva onto Main Street and into the great merchant heart of San Paolo. The Equinox's parking lot is almost empty, but it'll fill up tonight. Chelsea asked if I was going to the show and I told her hell no. Evermore and Fun Yung Moon aren't real bands. MTV pretty boys. Besides, fifteen bucks? I'll never get that Marshall if I waste my money on two bands I don't even like.

Goo and I went to the Equinox once together. We saw John Doe play with his band for a sold-out crowd. Awesome night. Goo didn't like the venue. They serve dinner before the show—dinner and a rock show. Can you believe it? Nothing more lame could ever exist on this or any other planet—and after the band went on the crowd just sat there, too bloated to dance or even stand. "Could've just as well gone to a morgue," Goo said, the 'R' curling around his lips.

But the band ruled. Fuckin' tight. The main man from X belted out songs in his throat-y croon, banged on his guitar, sweated right through his black T-shirt. I'd never heard of him, but Goo loved him, and I fell in love with him too. That night, I decided what I wanted to do with my life.

"A singer?" Goo said. His face twisted, like the time he accidentally drank cigarette ashes from a beer can. The band had just finished a number. Everyone was clapping.

"A punk singer," I said into his ear.

"A punk singer," he said. He smiled, ran his hand around the back of my neck and tugged me closer. The band broke into another song—a good, driving one to get those lame-os off their asses—and Goo leaned into me. He spoke so close to my ear I could feel his breath. "That's the best news I've heard for punk rock in a long time," he said.

I loved the son of a bitch more than ever for saying that. I treated him to something special right after the show. There's a perfect spot out by the parking lot, deep in the line of trees. When I got home Mom asked me how I got so dirty at an indoor concert. I told her she didn't want to know.

* * *

Thank god almighty I'm home at last.

Mom's BMW sits in our driveway, its platinum paint job losing its luster from too much sun. She can afford a new one. She used to be a hot shot advertising gal downtown, but since she quit a few months ago—to stay home and be "Mom" apparently—she doesn't feel the need to replace it. I told her the amp I want would cost about one one-trillionth of a new Beamer, but she just smiled that smile that says she wonders why she bothered to have a kid in the first place.

Even platinum loses its luster. There's a song in there. I have to remember it.

Mom's in the kitchen stirring something in a giant ceramic bowl. Her black sweat suit clings to her body, accenting her butt, which is flat as Plexiglas. Her ponytail—more of a little blond stump—moves, along with her butt, to the rhythm of the stirring. This new style doesn't look right on her. I was never crazy about the heels and blouses and frosted ends of her corporate life, but this soccer mom thing has to go. I want to grab her by the shoulders, shake her and scream, "What have you done with my mother?"

"Hel-lo," she chimes, doorbell-like, when she hears me sit down.

"Plotting to kill us off?" I say. Any attempt by Mom to cook can only be described as child and spousal abuse.

"Meaning what exactly?" she says. She turns towards me, her big, green eyes unblinking. Dark humor doesn't go over well with her anymore, which is quite a change from the crap she used to dish out. Since she quit work, she's been on a New Age kick, Yoga, Thai Chi. "Finally a chance to expand myself, to explore who I am," she said, but I don't buy it. I know she's home to keep an eye on me, the problem child who dropped out of school and might wind up in the gutter without her undivided attention.

"Nothing," I say. "What are you doing in there?"

"Whipping up a little something," she says.

"What?"

"Pasta dish," she says. "Your dinner."

"Not for me," I say. I stand up. "I've got to rock out with Stuart."

"No, you don't," Mom says. The singsong tone in her voice irks me, the calm tilt of her head. She knows something I don't. "Stuart stopped by today. He isn't going to be at band practice. He's going to a concert over at the Equinox."

"*What?*"

"He really wanted to see one of those bands. What are they called? Hong Kong Fuey?"

"Fun Yung Moon," I say. "Mom, you're kidding me."

"I'm not," Mom says. "Gladys is taking him."

"*Gladys?* No. Tell me he didn't go to the concert with his mother."

"What's wrong with going with his mom?" she says, even though she knows the answer. She goes back to stirring. "So I figured—since all three of us are going to be home for once—I would try to whip up something besides Pizza Chief. Doesn't that sound good?"

I watch her stir and know instantly I would rather eat a box of guitar picks than whatever's in that bowl. "I'm going out," I say. "I've got things to do."

"Betty," Mom yells, but I leave without answering.

* * *

Main Street—every street in this town leads to Main Street—is teeming with cars. It's after seven, and the burger I ate too fast is causing me stomach cramps. I could go home, but what would I do there? Watch the tube? Wait for tomorrow and the day after that and the day after that? I'd rather stay out. The buzz of my engine, *Rocket to Russia* on my stereo, at least this feels like progress.

The Equinox parking lot is almost full. Dinner must have started, a three-course meal they serve to justify the high ticket price. What a rip-off. And to think my drummer's in there, sitting across from his mom, eating a pork chop and waiting for some froo-froo rock band to give him the thrill of his life. I don't know how many times I've warned him. "This stuff can hook you in," I said, showing him my box of cassettes from my pre-punk days, Skid Row, Milli Vanilli and—I shutter to think now—Debbie Gibson. Stuart may be in too deep already. It's hard to stop people once they get going.

I tried to stop Goo.

On the day he left for good, he bought us a pizza from Galileo's. He tried to act like it was any other day, even though all his stuff was piled in his car, his apartment vacant. We sat and ate on the carpet of his living room.

"I'm pregnant," I told him.

"No, you're not," he said.

"I'm serious," I said. "I'm late. I haven't had it in weeks."

"Tell you what," he said. "You have the baby, and I'll send for you."

"But I don't want you to go at all," I said. I grabbed him around the neck. My tears fell on the buzzed part of his head. I squeezed him, unable to let go. "Who am I gonna talk to? I hate school. They're all just stupid kids."

"You'll be all right," he said. "Maybe we can hook up once you get out."

"You make it sound like prison."

"It is prison," he said, "but you'll get out. We all get out, one way or the other."

He left right after lunch, when workday traffic was thinnest. I hoped his Dodge Dart would break down and he would be forced to stay with me for one more day. I was still crying when Mom got home. I wouldn't tell her why.

* * *

A bow-tied lot attendant asks if I want valet service. Yeah, right.

I putter my Festiva through the rows and rows of cars. I'm going to this goddamn show tonight because there's absolutely nothing else to do in this god-forsaken town and it's the closest thing to something real I can find on short notice. I also have a sneaking suspicion I'm missing out on something, a feeling I could never stand. It's only fifteen bucks. Now that the dinner part's over I think I can stomach the rest.

I idle around the club, back to the line of trees where Goo and I shacked up way back when. The place will always hold a little magic for me, Goo shirtless on his back, the ground under my knees, sweat coming from every pore. It's probably why I took the job at Dart Mart. I could never feel too bad about going to work in the morning.

The bands' buses are parked behind the club. Ridiculously big. What do they think they're doing in tour buses? The Ramones toured their entire career in a van, and they're bigger than both of these bands combined. You'd think they thought they were the Rolling Stones or something.

I crank my Festiva into a parking spot along the line of trees. My headlights reveal someone just behind the branches. I see the eyes—scared—and a quick dodge to get out of sight.

I turn off the car. I always wondered if Goo would come back, come looking for me. I can't see anyone now, but there's definitely someone there. I hit my headlights and climb out. It's probably some transient, but I can't shake the sense that I know him. I step closer to the trees. I can make out someone just beyond, and I push back the branches. "Goo?" I say.

It's not Goo. It's the guy from Dart Mart who bought all the camping gear. He lies on his sleeping bag, motionless, looking like an escaped convict waiting out the posse. I thought he acted like he had something to hide. I guess this is it. "Sorry," I say. I let the branches go. "I thought you were someone else."

* * *

It isn't until later that I learn Fun Yung Moon's bass player is missing, and I'm the only one who knows where he is.

Life in the Bush

Fun Yung Moon went onstage. My band went onstage without me.

I can hear them playing, a song from our most recent record, "Stampede," a song I never liked. I focus on the bass playing. They must've dragged Fife to the back of the bus and crammed him full of bass lines. He's played okay so far. I didn't hear him screw up until the third song, "So Much Nothing," when he missed the C of the bridge and went straight to the F of the verse. I felt the dissonance all the way out here.

The cops showed up an hour ago. I watched Fife and Gad talk with them. Fife looked panicked, his arms gesturing, his hair messed up. Gad, in full gig attire—black, embroidered shirt, cowboy hat, shit-kickers—stood coolly by, arms crossed. I couldn't hear what was said, but they must've been talking about me. A few minutes before showtime and I hadn't shown up.

It feels like the first time I've heard these songs in years. You lose perspective when you're in a band, playing the same music night after night. You forget what you liked about it in the first place. When the band played "Carry Me," it reminded me of the first time Gad, Lance, and I practiced in Lance's living room, just before I left for Seattle. I love the simple hook of that chorus, Gad's scream, *Carry me away to someplace beautiful*.

There was a time when I loved playing in Fun Yung Moon more than anything. Our first gigs together felt like a gift from some higher being. Lance, Verge, Gad and I, we all sensed it. We'd found our purpose. Onstage I'd get so excited my head would start bobbing, my limbs would twitch. Everyone thought I looked possessed. Celia said after the first time she saw us, "You're quite the performer. For a second there I thought I was at a revival meeting."

That was it. There was a religious hitch to it. The music obliterated all that negative stuff—frustrations, second-guesses, insecurities. Their absence felt profound. I could've talked myself out of it, reminded myself how drunk and lightheaded I was, but why would I want to? I welcomed it. It beat the hell out of real life.

The main lot is full, and people have started to park around back by me. Out of nowhere, the Dart Mart girl showed up, Pippy Longstocking pigtails and all. I must've looked like a dork, lying on my belly, hoping she'd go away. *I thought you were someone else.* Sorry, kid. It's just me and—guess what?—I'm a little disappointed by that, too.

"You think too much," Verge once scolded me. He sat on the hotel bed next to mine, bright pills spread out before him, yellows, blues and pinks. "What you need is a good, prolonged drug habit. Have you smoked your marijuana today?"

The band's first single, "Nickel," had been catapulting up the charts, and all the attention made me nervous. Verge had given me four or five joints to calm me down, but after one hit of his kryptonite weed I wound up in my bed bunk, curled in the fetal position, trying to convince myself I wasn't going insane. "I don't like it," I told him. "It makes me paranoid."

"There's your problem," Verge said. "Ignore the paranoia. Focus on the colors and the shapes."

Verge is a lifelong rock 'n' roll rebel. He bought his ticket on the hellbound train years ago, and he's glad to still be enjoying the ride. No one knows how old he is, and he won't tell anyone. He has no past before Jejune July—his band with Gad in the early nineties—no family or friends, no driver's license. His laid-back style makes me think of him as my age, but the specks of gray in his hair suggest older. When Verge and I talk, it's like we're sharing a bus stop; there's nothing to do but chat, and compared to the other we'll each feel relatively sane.

Another time, the two of us cooped up in a hotel room in Baltimore, Verge asked, "What's with this stuff you're always reading?"

"What about it?"

He practiced guitar, played a lick high up on the neck of his Les Paul. I was bored, so I flipped through my copy of *Moby Dick*. "All of those words make you crazy," he said.

"Maybe it's everything else that makes me crazy."

He put his guitar facedown on his lap and leaned closer to me. Wrinkles splayed out from his eyes, trails of Fourth of July fireworks. "But it makes you so bass-ackwards with the rest of the world," he said. "Look at where you're at. Look at what we do. Nothing out here works like it does in books."

"Sure," I said. "Books are books, and real life is real life. Music isn't real life, either. Maybe we should quit listening to it."

"But music is *instinct*," he said. "You either like it or you don't. Books are words. You have to figure out what they're trying to say before you can know what you think about it."

"So, you're not against books," I said. "You're against struggling to get to the gist of them."

Verge shrugged his shoulders. "Why waste your time when there's so much truth right here?" He picked up his guitar and, eyes closed, played a slow blues lick.

"That's one kind of truth," I said. "There are others."

"Maybe," Verge said. "But do they feel this good?"

Inside, the band plays on, "Betroth," a song from *Fun Yung-Ola*, my favorite on the album. We rarely play it live. It's slow, but the simple progression, from E to D to C, gives the band a different dimension. It cuts against the radio-friendly package Gad is so into.

I love the flow of the music, the cascade down and back up of the chords, Forrest's hi-hat helping the rhythm along. The song pulls me away from myself, makes me feel distant from everything, reminds me how easy life can be if I just let it. *Why waste your time when there's so much truth right here?*

The first cool breeze of the night comes through the trees. It kindles a fear in me. There's something going on inside the club that I helped create, that reflects me, and I've given it up. That music was mine, and I ditched it. I've been rash, shortsighted. Fun Yung Moon was more than I ever dared hope for.

I came into the world of rock 'n' roll a pimply-faced high school kid with no illusions. Rock stars were, if not heroic, distinctly otherworldly. They stood at least six-feet-four. They wore spandex and had long hair that must've taken years to grow. And they had talent. David Lee Roth, Randy Rhoads, Neil Peart, I studied them all, watched videos, went to concerts. I wanted proof that they were once normal kids who had worked on their craft and one day sprouted rock 'n' roll wings. But my search came up empty. They were too perfect, too polished. I convinced myself that rock stars were born, not made. If you were one, you'd know it. I knew I wasn't.

And then times changed.

In 1991, mere months after I came back to Phoenix from Seattle, grunge broke across the country. Bands like Nirvana and Pearl Jam focused on loud, simple pop hooks. They ignored glitzy showmanship in favor of a down-to-earth sincerity. They wore thrift store clothes and had unkempt hair. All of a sudden, from MTV to our local clubs, people just like me populated the rock 'n' roll landscape. I could be one of them one day. Why not? They did it, and look at them. I had as good a chance as anyone.

Inside, the band breaks into "Nickel." It sounds a little slow— Fife might be dragging the bass line—but the crowd cheers louder than they have all night. Our signature song, the first song Gad played for me when I met him, our first single and our first hit. It brought listeners to Fun Yung Moon, got them to buy our CD and to come see us play. It brought paychecks from the record company, the publishing company, ASCAP. It bought cars and paid mortgages, acted as collateral for loans. It even got me out of a speeding ticket once. It's the main reason we're still out here on the road; sophomore flop or not, people still want to hear Fun Yung Moon play "Nickel." They probably always will.

I pull myself up and come out of the trees. I want to get closer to the music, to the center of this song, to see if it has one last message, one last lingering clue as to why I'm leaving it. Around back, away from the buses, a stack of cardboard boxes leans against a dumpster. The roof of the club comes almost to the ground, the rain gutter waist-high. I set my hands on the roof's shingles. I can feel it. The pop of the snare drum, the guitar, the rumbling bass. "Nickel." It's all there. Perfect rock.

I picture the four of them onstage, Gad commanding the scene like a ruler addressing his masses; Verge, head thrown back, smiling up to the sky; Forrest's workman-like pounding of the drums; Fife's mood swinging from wild euphoria to blind panic. In my vision of them, they all seem so ... *complete*. Their needs, all of them, are completely fulfilled by the band, this song, being onstage in front of these people. Gad gets the attention he feels he deserves. Verge continues his ride on the rock 'n' roll merry-go-round. Forrest keeps food on the table. Fife gets one last chance to rock the world. It's all they could ever want, all they could ever hope for. They play, the crowd cheers, and everybody's happy. Except me. "Nickel," for all its gifts, didn't bring me happiness.

The song ends, and I go back to my hiding place. I know—perhaps really know for the first time—that it's over for me and Fun Yung Moon. Tomorrow, the bus will drive to the Harvest Festival, taking my rock 'n' roll life with it.

Thursday

Sally

Something about the knock sounds like Illinois.

As soon as I hear it, the hair dryer still hot in my hand—before I can even think, "That's a knock at the door and that means someone's here"—I know it's not Marlon looking for his cat, or the paperboy with my late paper, or one of the kids from Guadalupe selling candy. The way the raps come, the easy syncopation—one two three—like their owner has all day to wait, I know it's somebody from my hometown. And after seeing Von a few days ago, I know it's Dale.

I set my hair dryer on the counter, stare at myself in the mirror. How different I'll look to him. The sixties locks are gone, replaced by a frayed perm that looks good in a scrambled sort of way. Permanent bronze skin. The age marks show, crow's feet, but I look pretty, damn it. I can make pretty out of nothing.

It was wrong, the way it all went down. He knows it, I know it, but something about that judgment twenty-some years later seems unfair. It was a different time, a different recipe for life. How a man and wife dealt with each other behind closed doors was their own business. I could've had him locked up for it, but I didn't want that. I wanted to run. I took our son, and I ran like hell.

I thump down the stairs, past the school photos of Josh *his son, my son* and I feel regret build in my stomach. It's going to be too much. The pictures, the years apart. What on earth can we say to each other? I should've let Von go by that day. I should've taken a pass on the whole thing and let everyone go on with their lives. But Josh deserves to know his dad. I take one last free breath before I swing the door open.

Dale looks smaller, shriveled, browner in the face. The drip of hair on his forehead has none of the sexiness it had when we were kids. His back curves slightly, the beginnings of an old man's stoop. I want to move this guy out of the way and see if the real Dale is behind him.

"Dale," I say, and I wrap my arms around him.

"Hey, Sally," he says. "You look good, girl."

"It's good to see you," I say.

"It's good to see you," he says.

Our hug—his palms on my back, the intervening years evaporating like rain—scares me, and I let go. "How long's it been?" I say.

"Oh," he says, sounding like his father, like all Midwesterners sound when they talk about the past. He looks like a farmer, brow wrinkled, counting the alternating years of corn and soy. "I guess it's been twenty-four, twenty-five years."

"Come on in," I say.

The kitchen's cluttered. I left the peanut butter unlidded on the counter. A frying pan I used to cook a grilled cheese last night sits on the stove, unclean. I could've given Von my phone number; a phone call would've given me a chance to prepare, but it also would've given me a way out. The address put it in his court. If he wanted to find us, he could find us.

Dale comes in, walks in his tennis shoes through my living room and sits on the couch without leaning back. It's as if he senses that I'm not entirely on board for this visit. His effort to keep straight and fly right—to keep his dirty shirt off the back of my couch—is almost sweet.

"So," I say. I sit in the pappa san, pull my feet up underneath me. This is the best I could've hoped for, Dale minding his 'P's and 'Q's on the couch, me all the way over here. We're barely in the same room. It's like watching a TV show starring him.

"So, how is he?" Dale asks. The crack in his voice, the nervous eyes, I want to protect him and protect myself *from* him at the same time.

"He's good, Dale," I say. "He's married. He's in a band that tours all over the country. He reminds me of you when he hooks his thumb in his pocket." I show him, hooking my thumb in my belt loop.

Dale laughs, just a little, and brings his hands together, the guilty thumbs touching. "What kind of band?"

"Rock, I guess," I say. "They're called Fun Yung Moon. I wouldn't be surprised if you've heard them. They had one song that was all over the radio a couple years ago. They played on *The Tonight Show*."

"You serious?" he says.

"You wouldn't've believed it," I say. "They played their song and the crowd went wild. Jay Leno shook Hote's hand right there on TV."

Dale looks confused. "Who?" he says.

"Jay Leno. You know, the host of *The Tonight Show*?"

"No," Dale says. "Who's Hote?"

And now I know it's coming. I never told him—how was I supposed to tell him if I didn't know where he was? And why would I track him down just to tell him something he didn't want to know? After a decade or so, all life mixing together, you forget about these things. Dale sits on the couch, his eyes focused on me. "I changed his last name to my family name, Dale," I say. "I changed it to Hotle. They call him Hote."

He sits there, looking down at his hands. He could be a monk praying if it weren't for those eyes. The blinks give him away.

"Well," he says. "I guess you can do whatever you want to do."

"It only seemed right," I say. "I changed my name back too. How am I supposed to explain to him we have different last names?"

"You can do whatever you want to do," he says, still not looking up. "What does he know about me?"

"He knows you exist," I say. "He knows we had a bad time of it."

"How does he know that?" he snaps. His thumbs push against each other.

"How do you think he knows?" I say. I stare back at him. It suddenly hits me that this man doesn't belong here, that he brings nothing to the table, that this dirty T-shirt in my living room offers only chaos and confusion. But we can't start fighting already. Once we start, we'll never stop. "Listen," I say. "You don't have to worry about anything. We didn't get into specifics."

This brings him back to earth a little. "When can I see him?" he asks.

"He's on tour right now," I say, "but he'll be back in a week."

"Where're they on tour?"

"I'm not sure," I say. I move to grab a pen from the coffee table. "You can find out anything you want at their web site."

"I don't have a computer, Sally," Dale says, and he stands up, his visit abruptly over. He's developed a quickness, a headstrong pursuit, that he didn't have before, like life blows against him all the time and the only way he knows to get anywhere is to push back.

"Well, I have a one upstairs," I say.

* * *

We walk up together, past the pictures of Josh that line the stairway, the third grade one in his basketball jersey, the awkward one from sixth grade in his yellow Izod, the graduation shot with the mullet and earring.

"He's a lot like you," I say, but thinking *he's as much not as he is*.

"How do you mean?"

"Well, he thinks a lot, and he's never real sure about life, like he's always stepping on a frozen pond and wondering if he's gonna fall through. He's never satisfied, I guess is what I mean."

"You think I'm never satisfied?"

I'm suddenly conscious of him behind me, his thumping presence following me up the stairs. If he wanted to hurt me, now would be the time. "I wouldn't know," I say. "It's been awhile."

I lead him to the computer room, which used to be Josh's bedroom. Sunlight angles through the French doors that lead out to the balcony. The room feels dusty, even though I just cleaned it. One side of the closet is full of Josh's stuff from childhood—a baby book, awards from grade school, teenage junk—but I don't want to mention it or I'll never get out of here. I sit down at the computer, wake it with a shake of the mouse. "The band has a great web site," I say. The modem clicks on, and the dial tone buzzes into the room.

Dale stands in the doorway, a skinny, nervous mass, wondering if he should come in. "Listen," he says. "I don't want you to think I'm hangin' around. I'm just lookin' to get in touch with Josh."

"It's all right," I say. The computer's making all kinds of noise, and I turn it down.

"I mean," Dale says. "You got every right to hate me."

"I don't hate you," I say, which may or may not be true. Either way, it's not a conversation I want to have with him. Too much information given up too early. The computer's taking forever.

"I mean," he says. He takes a step into the room. "You gotta admit I was—it was pretty fucked up."

He can't be talking about the last night. I feel my stomach sink, and my hand shakes on the mouse. "Oh?" is all I can think to say.

"You know," he says. "The way it ended. It was . . . it was wrong."

I shake the mouse, trying to get something to happen on the screen. *It can't matter after all these years, but it does. I feel like it does.*

"I just want you to know," he says. "I know whose fault it is, and it isn't you and it isn't Josh." I feel my stomach quiver. "Know what I mean?"

"Yes," I say, but knowing full well that's not the whole story. *I took your son. I took him for twenty years. If I hadn't run into Von that day, I would've taken him forever.* The tears come, balloons filling with water at the corners of my eyes.

The browser window pops open. "There it goes," I say, a little too quickly, wiping my eyes with my hand. I go to my favorites and find Fun Yung Moon's address.

Dale comes up behind me. "Where they playin'?" he asks.

"Let me find it," I say. I can't believe I let myself cry. Twenty years on my own and nothing. This guy's back in my life for ten minutes and I'm blubbering all over myself again. I go to the tour page and find the concert listings. In one corner, a picture of the band, Josh, his full lips, peering over Gad's shoulder. The dates are below. "They played Orange County last night," I say. "Today it's Fresno. The fairgrounds. I can print off the address if you want."

"No," he says. "I'll find it, but print off that picture."

No Fun Intended

Last night I dreamed of my dad.

I don't know much about him. He cooked at a restaurant where my mom waitressed. She was eighteen, just out of high school. He was "older." When she got pregnant with me, they gave each other a try. "He didn't want to give you up," Mom told me.

Mom gets nervous when I ask about him, answers quickly and scurries away. I've made a point not to bother her about it. Once, I eavesdropped on her phone conversation with my aunt and heard her say, "If he weren't Josh's dad, I would've had him thrown in jail." I hate to think of my mom in harm's way, and I guess I blame him for that. "He did drugs" is all she'll say.

In my dream my dad and I walk along a dirt road. There's a town up ahead, a clump of trees and a church steeple, and we both move quickly to get to it. My dad hands me, of all things, a violin case. I take the case without a word and keep walking towards the town. I feel proud that we're doing this together, my dad and me, that he trusts me with the violin case.

And then I woke up, my pride melting into daybreak.

For being outside and in the middle of a business district, it wasn't a bad night's sleep. I woke up a few times, once when a semi drove down Main Street, once when a flock of birds landed in the bush next to me. My neck hurts, and I have no idea where I'll take my next shower, but today is all mine. Low clouds, probably from the ocean, creep above the trees.

I hear a car pull into the Equinox parking lot, the first car of the morning. It putters right up to the trees and parks just a few yards away. The idling sounds close. Someone gets out and pushes through the trees.

"You still here?"

It's that girl, the Dart Mart girl. This—the third time we've crossed paths in less than a day—can't be a mistake. Someone or something is putting this girl in front of me. A prize, a message, a sacrifice, I don't know which. "I'm still here," I say.

The Pippy Longstocking 'do is gone, her red hair pulled back in a vague, bobby-pinned way over her ears. She wears a white blouse and a plaid, pleated miniskirt. She'd look like a Catholic schoolgirl if it weren't for her body—thin waist, ample chest.

"I know who you are," she says.

"Who am I?"

"You're the guy who quit Fun Yung Moon."

"What makes you say that?"

She shifts her weight. Her combat boots make her feet look big, like Minnie Mouse. "Their bass player scrammed on them last night," she says. "I saw you out here, and I put two and two together."

"And what did it add up to?"

"That you were the guy," she says. She points with an overturned hand gesture.

"How do you know I'm not a transient?"

"You're too clean," she says. "Too sane-looking."

"It's good to know I'm sane-looking," I say, "even though I'm not exactly clean right now. You got me, I'm the guy."

"I knew it," she says. She claps once, scaring some birds from the trees. "I saw you out here last night, and I knew there was something going on."

"So, you won," I say. "What would you like to claim as your prize?"

She looks at me, nibbles her thumb. There's an aura of freshness about her, of actions and mannerisms that haven't been repeated a million times. She reminds me of Lance's drumming, brash, direct, always a little ahead of the beat. She can't be more than sixteen. "What are my choices?" she asks.

"Name it," I say. "But I need to keep this quiet, so consider it hush money, too."

"Okay," she says. "I guess I wanna know why you quit your band."

"Good question," I say. "I'm not sure I can answer it."

"You wanna go somewhere with me?" she asks. "I'd really like to know."

* * *

Her car is a little blue something-or-other. Really small. I have to kick garbage out of the way to make a place for my feet. Despite the mess, the car smells girlish. Body wash, maybe Aqua Net.

Raoul used Aqua Net. He was the lead singer for Witch Hunt, a metal band Lance and I joined after our senior year. Before every gig, Raoul stacked his long, black locks over his head, mane-like, and shellacked it there with enough Aqua Net to challenge hurricane force winds. "Makes me look taller," he'd say, making up for his five-feet-seven frame. During the set, he liked to show off his martial arts moves, and by the end of the night his hair would edge down one side of his head, looking like the sad, drooping body of a wounded animal. His voice, thin and screechy, only accented this sense of dying prey. Still, Lance and I stuck it out in Witch Hunt for the whole summer. Any band was better than no band.

"I'm in a band, too," she says.

"Really," I say. I don't know if I can muster the energy to encourage her. I'm pretty far from the carefree days of Witch Hunt right now. If she tries to give me a demo tape I swear I'll throw it out the window.

"We're in the beginning stages," she says, "but I've got a drummer and a whole bunch of songs. We're gonna be called No Fun Intended. I had a lawyer check it out. It's not taken."

"Cool," I say. We pass a Ford dealership, the windshields of trucks reflecting the morning clouds. "So, have a good time with it. The good part doesn't last forever."

"What do you mean?" She shifts to a higher gear, speeds up to catch a light before it turns red.

"Things get old," I say. "You think you have to take it to the next level to keep it alive, but that pretty much guarantees you'll kill it."

"Well, that's not gonna happen to me," she says. "I quit high school to get this band going, and I'm totally focused on making it work."

"You dropped out of high school to start a band?" I say. "You couldn't finish *while* you played in a band?"

She stops at a red light, tires screeching. "Listen," she says. She leans towards me, points at her own chest. I think I pissed her off. "This here's no high school girl. I've got the songs, I've got the talent, and I'm not wasting my time in Algebra class learning the *foil* method, or in art class gluing macaroni to construction paper, or in lunchrooms with jocks trying to see up my skirt. I know who I am and I know what I want, so forgo the guidance counselor bullshit with me. I get enough of it from everyone else."

"Gotcha," I say.

The light turns green and we go.

"So, I'm Hote," I say. "I don't suppose you have a name to go with all that angst."

"I have a name," she says, "but I'm not sure I'm going to tell you."

"Okay. I've been calling you Pippy Longstocking since yesterday. I'll just call you Pippy."

"Pippy," she says. "I like it, but who the hell's Pippy Longstocking?"

* * *

Bowling alleys always shock my system, the colors and shapes something out of a barrel of sherbet ice cream. Who made the decision to have every bowling alley look some kid's Easter morning nightmare? Is it an obligation to keep up appearances, or does every owner just have bad taste? You'd think one day, if only by accident, a bowling alley would crop up with mellow, sane colors. They'd probably get run out of town, or have their red pin privileges revoked.

Pippy and I are at Earthquake Alleys. Pippy faces our lane, her body surrounded by the pastel swirls of the decor. The curves of the decor match the curves of Pippy, the slope of her neck and shoulders as she holds the ball, the incline of her hair, her waist and legs. It strikes me that I'm on what could be mistaken as a date with her—a twenty-six-year-old out with a teenager—and I scan the place to make sure no one pays too much attention. The smiling guy behind the counter doesn't care. A distracted blue-jeaned kid waxes the lanes. No customers, just us. We're free to bowl, chat, let the day take us where it may.

Pippy eases forward—one step, two—and ends up on her tiptoes. She takes two hurried steps as her ball eases back. Her arm cuts through the air, and she releases the ball, her right foot sliding gracefully behind her. The ball angles towards the gutter and slopes back, heads for the pocket. *Crash.* Pins go everywhere. Strike. She strolls back to me.

"What's your high score?" I ask.

"Two-oh-four," she says. She sits on one of the contoured chairs and crosses her legs. I love watching her, the swoops of her body, the teasing way she flicks one leg over the other. She was born to be looked at, a punk Annette Funichello. "I was in a league in junior high that toured all over California. I've got trophies."

"So what's all this about playing music?" I say. "Sounds like you could be a pro bowler."

She looks at me like I have three heads. Her look makes me feel older, and I'm glad for it. She's young, sexy, probably talented, and she has two strikes on the board; my age is my only leverage. "Bowling?" she says. "You've got to be kidding. Who would want to be a bowler when you could–" She stops, rolls her eyes. "Oh. You, probably."

"What's wrong with bowling?" I say. I'm not up for painting a nice, rosy picture of life in rock 'n' roll for her. If she thinks she's different than the rest of us, she'll have to prove it to me. "You get to tour the country, just like a musician. You get your own entourage. You can create your own line of bowling shoes, your name engraved on each one."

"I don't play music to get famous," she says. "That's the difference–" She stops. *Between you and me,* she wanted to say.

I should've seen it coming. How could I have missed it? The crazy get-ups, the punk rock cassettes in her car. She thinks Fun Yung Moon is lame, and that's fine, but I'm not willing to let her off that easily. "And you think I played music to get famous?" I say. "To be on MTV? To play places like the Equinox and to sign autographs after the show? Listen, music was all that mattered to me at your age."

"*At my age,*" she says, rolling her eyes again.

"Yes," I say. "*At your age.* There's nothing wrong with being your age, and there's nothing wrong with things changing as you get older. In fact, you can count on it."

She looks away. I've lectured her, and she's turned off. "You haven't even heard my songs," she says.

Within the pout lurks an invitation. *Come somewhere with me. We'll listen to my songs and see where it leads us.* The abruptness of her offer startles me. "Later," I say, trying to sound uninterested. "First, I'm gonna take care of you on the lanes."

I pick up my ball. The pins await, dumb to my intentions.

"I've been meaning to tell you," Pippy says. "You need to keep your head straight when you—"

"Cool it," I say, not taking my eyes off the pins. I'm going to throw the ball right through them, knock every one of them over and pump my fist in the air. I take one step and ease the ball back, my eyes focused on the foul line. Two hurried steps and I let it fly.

Unlike Pippy's ball, mine has almost no steer to it, going straight for the center of the pins with no curve. It angles just a bit and hits the opposite side of the head pin. When the rubble clears, one pin on the far end is standing. I missed the strike, but something in the throw says I won't be a pushover for the rest of the game. I can hold my own, even against future-pro Pippy Longstocking.

"Wham-o," she says. "I thought that last one was gonna fall for a second."

"I missed the pocket," I say. "I didn't deserve a strike."

"The best strikes are the undeserved ones," she says. "How are you at the seven-pin?"

"We're gonna find out."

I have to bowl cross-lane, which means I can't throw it as hard as I want. I grab my ball and set myself up on the far right dot. The lone pin, a prisoner awaiting execution, stands by. My approach is less hurried, and I bowl deliberately, almost setting the ball on the lane.

I can tell instantly I've missed. The ball angles left too quickly and goes straight into the gutter. I aimed too much, tried to control it. Another open frame. Pippy's gonna cream me.

"That shot's not as easy as—"

"Oh, shut up," I say.

* * *

"What's so awful about it?" Pippy asks.

After being mauled by her on the lanes—it wasn't even close despite my twenty-seven in the tenth—we meandered over to the Earthquake burger joint and ordered lunch. TVs occupy every space, each replaying some sporting event or other. Baseball, basketball, horse racing, it's hard to keep up with it all. We're the only people in here save the restaurant staff, who are busy setting up for lunch.

I set my burger down. After a night of nothing but Chips Ahoy, bowling alley food hits the spot. "Nothing, really," I say. "It's all so cliche it's hardly worth mentioning."

"Oh, come on," she says. "You're the only person I've ever met from the other side. Give me some gossip at least."

"That's the whole problem," I say. "When you're young, you have your life, and you see this other life through TV and movies and magazines, and you think, 'That's where the good life must be lived,' because the one you're living sure isn't."

Pippy nods, chews her burger. Her big, green eyes shine like coins at the bottom of a fountain. Wishes.

"And then you grow up," I say. "You learn that the world of pop culture isn't some Holy Grail of happiness. But now your dreams are all tied up with it, and you have no real sense of what else to do. Those lucky enough to make the big time tend to stick with it, milk it for all its worth. Some people drop out, get a job, start a family."

"And then there's people like you," Pippy says.

"—who don't really believe in any of those paths but are still trying to find a life worth living, hoping there's one out there. What else can you do?"

Pippy drains her soda with one quick suck of her straw. "Here's what you do. You forget all that stuff and rock out. Come on. I've got something I want to show you."

* * *

Her bedroom is more Barbie than Bosstones. Pink chiffon bed overhang, vanity mirror, white dresser with moldings, along with the usual teenage stuff. The smell, a nice combination of unclean linen and shampoo, must come from her bed. "Someone went to a lot of trouble to make you feel like a girl," I say.

"I know," she says. She gets down to retrieve her guitar from under the bed. There's something both tough and sexy about her, and the combination, combined with being alone with her in her house, in her bedroom, has me thinking thoughts I probably shouldn't. "Believe it or not," she says, "I picked it out myself when I was nine. I protested for a while, but now I kind of like it again. It's perverse in a K Records sort of way."

She flips open her guitar case and pulls out the best looking Gretsch hollow-body I've ever seen. Fat cherry-red body, rosewood neck, F-holes. It shines as she sits on her bed and hikes it onto her knee.

"Girl," I say. "Where did you get the money for that?"

"Same as everything else," she says. "Dad pays for it." She flicks through a few bar chords, sliding her hand up, up, up the neck, the pitch getting higher and higher. "He came to his senses when I asked for a new amp. He likes the guitar, but something about a Marshall scares the shit out of him."

"I can see his point."

"So," she says. It hits her that she's auditioning for me, and all the lights in her eyes go on. "What do you want to hear, a slow one or a fast one?"

"Your best one," I say. "How 'bout a slow one?"

"Okay," she says, and she breaks into a nice descending arpeggio lick. She struggles to get it right, screws it up a little, and smiles a smile that could break a million little boys' hearts. She slides her hand down into an open chord.

> It all came down to a quarter of a dollar
> That I was saving for my finest hour
> That all your money and all your power
> Could never take away from me

> Some forget the power of a penny
> With some so few and some so many
> You think your friends are all your enemies
> Who want to take away from you

Her hand slides back up the neck, and she picks the arpeggio lick again.

"That's nice," I say.

She doesn't look up. She's concentrating. The lick's clearer this time.

> All alone with your random bullshit
> A boring game show, an overplayed pop hit
> All I want is to make you stay put
> But you'll never make me say it

> Someone starts and others go on
> And the radio plays my favorite pop song
> The one I wanted to hear all along
> But you'll never make me show it

"Great," I say. "So, where's the chorus?"

She looks up quickly and back down, a sign I should be patient.

> And the radio keeps playing
> And your words keep saying
> That nothing really matters anymore
> That you're the only one
> Never meant to be

"Wow," I say. "Wow, Pip. That's really good. That's actually scary good."

She stops. She wants to go on, but the flattery is getting to her.

"It's called 'Never Meant to Be,'" she says. She sets the guitar face down on her lap. "Do you really like it?"

"I do," I say. "You sound like a female Paul Westerberg. Get the right agent and I could see you touring with–"

Suddenly, Pippy's eyes grow big and she stands up. "Say Lisa Loeb and the maid vacuums up your teeth tomorrow."

"Pip," I say, laughing a little. "There's nothing wrong with your songs being a little sweet. No one's gonna think you're not punk enough."

She sets her guitar on the bed and walks to the window. She's not sure how she feels about this. The sentiments are all right there, but she's got an image to protect. "You think I give a shit what other people think?" she says.

"Yes, I do," I say. She stands at the window, a muted light silhouetting her. I ease my way over. "We all care a little about what other people think. If we didn't we'd be sociopaths." I come up behind her, close enough to smell her, a combination of skin and hairspray. She acts unaware of me, but I sense the tension in her body, the way she moves and doesn't move, the give and take of the air around us. I slide my hands over her shoulders, feel her muscles through her blouse.

A light tick—then another, then some more—comes from above. The ticking grows into a constant pattering. It's rain. Rain hits the roof, breaking the moment.

"Cool," Pippy says, moving away from me. "I can't remember the last time it rained here."

"Me, either."

"I'm going outside," she says, and she bounds out of the room and down the stairs.

Good Christ. Three years on the road, three years with girls around all the time, and now I'm coming on to some high school girl in her pink chiffon bedroom? I'm embarrassing myself. I don't belong here. Her parents could come home any minute.

The front door opens and closes.

I'll get out of here. I'll apologize, I'll say my goodbyes, and get the hell out of here for good. There's no way I could let that happen. She's just a kid.

I climb down the stairs and catch a glimpse of her through the window in the front door. She stands on the lawn, her arms outstretched, her hands flat to catch the rain. It pops her on the palms, the shoulders, the head, little missiles that do no damage. She hops her way over to one of the two trees in the front yard and swings around it like Fred Astaire. She follows up with some knee-bending punk dance and shakes her head in a way that would give me whiplash.

I put my hand on the windowsill. It's a portal to another world. I'm looking out at something familiar but lost to me. It *is* me. The bowling alley, the Aqua Net, the self-consciousness, the punk cassettes in the car. It's my past, my adolescence flaunting itself in front of me. It doesn't care if it's a happy memory for me, or sad, or dull, or depressing. It just is. It's out there, and I'm in here.

Pippy sees me looking at her and motions for me to come out. I hold up my hand, no. The rain comes harder, but she's determined to stay out there for as long as she can, until she falls over or gets soaking wet or is struck by lightning. I'm determined to watch her. I can see nothing beyond it, beyond a dancing, wet Pippy in the front yard in the rain.

Digs

It's all gone, the Tempe streets I could barely see, the bar maids who knew my tricks, the broken down Buick in the parking lot where I sat and drank and watched the blur of cars go by. I thought I was giving up rock 'n' roll. Fuckin' fate. Rock 'n' roll is all I got.

What can I say about Rock 'n' Roll Heaven? How 'bout I could live without the whole thing. Morrison with his bunk poetry, Elvis on the throne, Sid moaning "Nancy, Nancy." There are plenty of places to play. All the good, dead rock clubs are here. I went to the Sun Club last night and saw D. Boon play solo acoustic. He banged out CCR covers, broke into classical interludes. It was the best thing I've heard in a long time, the best night I've had since I've been up here, that's for sure.

Phil Lynott, the dead bass player from Thin Lizzy, explained the rules to me when I got here. He sat me down after my introductory jam—yes, you get to jam with everyone on your first day. Jimi, Keith Moon, Buddy Holly. It was fine, I guess. I could've skipped the whole thing, to tell you the truth, but I'd just gotten here and I was kind of a mess and I didn't have the spirit to say no.

Anyway, Lynott explained the rules to me. "Rule number one, righ'," he said. He's got this thick Irish accent, which is kind of weird coming from a black guy. "Rule number one is no drugs or alcohol."

I about fell off my cloud right there. "What kind of rock 'n' roll heaven is this?" I said.

Lynott kind of laughed, but he kind of didn't, too. "Drugs and alcohol got most of us 'ere," he said. "It was decided long ago that Rock 'n' Roll 'eaven would have no drugs and no alcohol. You think otherwise? Go talk to Bonzo. Even he swore off the stuff."

"Good for him," I said, "but rock 'n' roll *wouldn't be* rock 'n' roll without drugs and alcohol. It's part of the deal. You can't just take it out. I wrote 'Piece of Luck' smashed out of my mind."

"Piece o' wha'?" Lynott said.

"'Piece of Luck,'" I said. "It's after your time. You've probably never heard it."

"Well," he said, smiling, "let's assume rock 'n' roll would get by without *Piece o' Luck*." He laughed a little. I vowed right there to stay away from him. "Rule number two." He wasn't wasting any time with me. "You're allowed no women in Rock 'n' Roll 'eaven."

"What?" I said. "No women?"

"No women in Rock 'n' Roll 'eaven," he said. I shit you not. He used those exact words.

"Well, that just can't be," I said. "How in the hell can Rock 'n' Roll Heaven not have any women?"

"They break up the bands," Lynott said. He was getting tired of me, I could tell, twiddling this medallion dangling from his neck— total Hendrix rip-off, by the way. I think he's getting sick of having to be the one to break the bad news. "We're all still a little pissed about the whole Yoko thing," he said, "and that was before Courtney Love. It's to the point that John and Kurt don't even argue anymore."

"You have a point with Courtney and Yoko," I said. "But absolutely no women? Besides the obvious problems, what about Janis Joplin? You can't keep her out of Rock 'n' Roll Heaven, can you?"

"Janis is 'ere," Lynott said, "but she's a nun now."

"A nun?"

"Once she got off the booze she saw the ligh'," Lynott said.

"Great," I said. "Janis is a nun. That's great. Would you mind showing me the way to the rock 'n' roll gun closet?"

"There's one more thing," he said. "Rule number three. In Rock 'n' Roll 'eaven, no drummas are allowed to jam with no other drummas."

"Why not?" I asked. I'd never been in a band with two drummers, and I had no desire to be in a band with two drummers, but I had to hear the reason.

"We don't like all the racket," he said. "If you're gonna play the drums, play with someone else, or play by yourself, but don't just bang aroun'—clankety-clank—with another drumma. It's annoyin'."

I leaned back into my cloud—incidentally, it feels a lot like a beanbag chair—and put my hands behind my head. "I can't believe this bullshit," I said. "You mean to tell me there's no sex or drugs in Rock 'n' Roll Heaven?"

"And no drummas bangin' around with no other drummas," Lynott said.

"Who gives a shit about the drummers?"

"Jerry Garcia, for one," he said. "He was pretty pissed at first, but he's comin' aroun'."

"Well," I said, "you've managed to take all of the fun out of rock 'n' roll for me. What exactly do I get out of the deal?"

Lynott leaned into me. His eyes got real big, and he seemed for the first time to take an interest. "You get to rock out, righ'," he said, smiling. "You get to rock out all the fuckin' time."

So, the whole thing's a little depressing for me, as you can imagine. I've got a room with all these rock 'n' roll things around me. Rock 'n' roll bed, rock 'n' roll rug, rock 'n' roll cloud beanbag chair, every guitar and bass and drum you can imagine stuffed away in a rock 'n' roll closet. The rock 'n' roll television plays all the concerts and videos that ever existed. Every band has its own channel. Even *Krokus!* Krokus TV. *Good Christ!*

But I act like it isn't even there. I act like it's all a bad painting in a cheap motel room in a lame city where the bars close too early. So, what do I do in Rock 'n' Roll Heaven to keep myself busy, with all these rock 'n' roll amenities at my disposal? I read. I sit on my bed and read classic books—Henry Miller, Harry Crews, Bukowski—all day and all night. That's the one good thing about dying and going to Rock 'n' Roll Heaven; all of your ailments go away. My eyesight's back. No more struggling to see the words. I read my favorites, and when I'm done I read them over again. It's as close to heaven as I get up here.

But I'd trade it all right now for a girl to come to my room, someone I recognize from somewhere but who I can't quite place. She'd bring a bottle with her, some grass. "Snuck it in," she'd say. She'd offer to roll a joint, but I'd tell her not to bother, point to the bottle. We'd split it right here in my room and spend the rest of the night in bed. I'd fall asleep with her against me, and I'd wake up the next day to the smell of breakfast cooking. I'd be so thankful I'd write a song for her.

And do I miss playing music? Sure. Not the Angels, but sometimes I hear the scratch of chords from a distant room somewhere in these halls. I picture some kid leaning over an acoustic guitar, banging out G and C and D chords, trying to make something worth having. I almost want to go help him, show him a different way to finger the G so it doesn't ring so much, offer a melody for the chorus, maybe a fourth chord for the bridge. I can imagine, with a little help, our song turning into the most heart-wrenching three minutes you've ever heard, and I'd go find Lynott. I'd grab him by that phony little medallion of his, pull him close to me and say, "You hear that? That plaintive little attempt at bliss? *That's* rock 'n' roll heaven. Keep at it, and maybe you'll get there someday."

Octave's

"It's the best place in town to get an amp," Pippy says. "Just don't let Octave talk you into lessons. Those hippies in back don't know shit."

We're driving to Octave's, a music store in Santo Domingo, which is the industrial yang to San Paolo's yin. Long grain-elevator-like tubes slant a hundred feet in the air. Mountains of sand and rock sit behind chain-link fences. It's funny how suburban areas try to hide the "less desirable" sections of town. You wouldn't know this place was back here unless you lived here, and it actually injects some life into Orange County for me. Trucks roll, people get to work.

Pippy leads me to a set of glass double doors and pulls one open. After her rain dance she changed into a baggy gray sweatshirt that says "Titans" across the front, but she stuck with the Catholic schoolgirl skirt. The chemistry between us has changed since our moment in her bedroom. She's more likely to touch me, to act coy, to hang back in her actions long enough to let me look. She insisted that I come see the amp she wants to buy.

"Pippy," I say as I walk through the door. She makes a point of sticking her boobs out as I walk past her. "Do you know how many Marshall half stacks I've seen in my life?"

"I know," she says. "It never gets tiring, does it."

The store, off-white walls, tiled floor, looks like it must have been a Laundromat at one time, and a hint of detergent smell still remains. The room is awash in amplifiers, stacked two and three deep to the walls and in the center. A thin path meanders to the counter. A ponytailed man talks on the phone, waves distractedly at Pippy. Another man, younger, bigger, with long, raven-colored hair coming from under his Angels cap, squats on a stool and plays bass guitar. I recognize the bass line as "Crazy Train." He plays with a greedy, breathless air about him, like if he stops for a even one second he might be asked to leave.

"Say, girl," the guy behind the counter says. He hangs up the phone. "You come to get your amp?"

"Hey, Octave," Pippy says. "Not yet. Just making sure you're taking care of it."

"Good as new," he says. He comes out from behind the counter. He has a slight hitch to his walk, like one leg is shorter than the other. Still, he moves quickly, leans forward, his ponytail bouncing. "Who's your boyfriend?"

Pippy glances at me, grins. "Octave, you're the only man for me."

"Sure, you say that now," he says. He leads us to a different part of the store. "But once you get that amp you're gonna be gone. Love 'em and leave 'em, that's your type."

"Ignore him," Pippy says to me. "He's been cranky ever since David Lee Roth got thrown out of Van Halen."

"He *quit*," Octave says. "David Lee Roth *quit* Van Halen."

He goes behind a row of amps and places his hand on top of a Marshall half stack, JCM800. "Here she is," he says. "Same as you left her."

"See?" Pippy says. She pokes me in the ribs and hustles over to the amp. She poses next to it, passes her hand over it like a hostess on *The Price is Right*. "Isn't it cool?"

"Very cool," I say, and I mean it. New amps always look great. Polished vinyl, shiny knobs, no dings or scratches. My amp—the one

Fife's probably soundchecking right now in Fresno—is a mess. The gig light on top broke years ago. Two knobs disappeared somewhere. The black vinyl of the cabinet looks like a large jungle animal got to it. "You gotta get a Les Paul if you want that crunch tone," I say. "How's it gonna sound with your Gretsch?"

"Billy Duffy of the Cult used Gretsch and Marshall on *Electric*. It sounds great."

"So, Billy," Octave says. "You wanna play it some, or did you just come by to gawk?"

"Got your Gretsch here?" she asks.

"My Gretsch stays at home, dear," he says. "Nothing comes in here that I don't want to get stolen. If you like, I got the Epiphone in back."

"I'll pass," she says. She stares at her amp. "I just wanted to show it to Hote. You know, he's famous, Octave. He plays bass—or he used to—in Fun Yung Moon."

"No kidding," Octave says. He scans me. "Son of a bitch. Why didn't you say so? I would've been nicer to him from the start. You were in Fun Yung Moon?"

It's the first time anyone has referred to my life in Fun Yung Moon in the past tense, and it scares me a little. I suddenly feel adrift. "I'm just on break," I say.

"A real pro in my humble abode," Octave says. "We normally don't get your kind here. See that guy?" He points to the kid playing bass guitar, who's moved on to a song by Yes, "Roundabout," a quick percussive lick I could never quite handle. "Pedro comes in here every day. No job, no girl. All he's got in this world are the clothes on his back and his ability to play bass guitar. He knows every song ever written, sits there and plays them over and over again, and do you know what he thinks about while he's playing?"

"I know exactly what he thinks about," I say. I remember my trips to Beardsley's as a teenager, hanging out all day, bugging the salesmen. "He thinks about how cool it would be to be in a band as famous as Fun Yung Moon."

"I see guys like him all the time," Octave says. "And they all want the same thing, to be as far along as you are. A few get there, the rest come here."

"Octave's band almost got signed in the eighties," Pippy says, half paying attention. She squats to look at the back of the Marshall head.

"We were this close," Octave says. He holds his thumb and forefinger together, uprights for an impossible field goal. "We had the players, the singer, a song the metal kids would go nuts for called 'The Rockin' at the Top.' The president at Combine Records was ready to ink us. You know what killed it?"

"What?"

"The drummer," he says. "The night of our showcase gig, our drummer didn't show up. He didn't call, didn't relay a message, just didn't show up. The rest of us waited, ready to play for these people who were gonna sign us, who had a contract sitting on the table along with their drinks, but we had no drummer. We called his work, his place, had our set pushed back. Didn't matter. Complete no-show."

"Did you ever see him again?" I ask.

Octave shakes his head. "He still hasn't come back, as far as I know. His girlfriend thought he got kidnapped. Everyone had their theory, but I think I know what really happened." Octave leans closer to me. One lock of black hair, loose from his ponytail, slopes down his forehead. "I remember all those times he got picked on for dragging the beat, or got shit from the lead singer, or had to play what someone else told him instead of what he wanted to play, and it finally pissed him off enough. I think, in his way, he was trying to tell us that it wouldn't work, that we would've eventually killed each other. I think he thought he was doing us a favor." Octave smiles, slides a finger across an amp. "Don't do me any favors."

"Well, I can see you're taking good care of it," Pippy says. She puts the amp head back in place, stumbling as the weight tries to pull her over. "With any luck I'll have the money by Christmas."

"It'll be here," Octave says. "Or one just like it. There's no shortage of Marshall amps in this world."

* * *

Our drummer disappeared, too. Lance's disappearance was more gradual, but it was the same, deliberate process of someone removing themselves from your life. Just as Fun Yung Moon started to get interest from record labels, Lance started hanging out with his old friends from the frat house, guys who drove nice cars and never seemed at a loss for money. He arrived at our gigs right before we went onstage, and he left right after we finished. He had no opinion about things like band practice or set lists or even which label we should sign with. He had little to say about anything, except for the occasional rant about people spying on him or tapping his phone or stealing his stuff. I didn't believe the rumors. Meth just wasn't his style. We'd grown up together, Lance and me, and I'd never known him to try anything harder than pot. On a trip to play for some industry types in Los Angeles, he revealed his secret to me.

"Come up to my room," Lance said. "I got this thing. You're gonna love it."

We walked up the stairs of the Firebird Hotel and went into his room. Our trips to different cities—flown to New York or Los Angeles or Nashville to play showcase gigs—were becoming regular happenings. It was only a matter of time before all bids would be in and we could make a decision. Lance and I were on the verge of getting everything we'd ever wanted, a mutual high school dream fulfilled, but by the way he acted you'd think we were forcing him to do it.

Lance drew the curtains, turned all the lights on, the TV, and pulled his knapsack out from under the bed. He took out a glass pipe that looked like something from a scientist's laboratory. The glass twisted and turned, forming what could have been a model of human intestines. A small, silver bowl stuck out the middle, and a place for your mouth poked out the top. Lance wrapped his lips around it, sucking, making the water in the intestines rattle. He looked at me with excited eyes. "You like?" he asked.

"You've come a long way since the dragon bong," I said.

"And it hits so smooth," he said. He took another suck. "I can't tell you how good it makes me feel. The first time—" He set the bong down on the table and took from his pocket a balled-up piece of aluminum foil. "It was like being awake for the first time in a long time."

I said nothing, watched him withdraw a salt-white nugget from the foil and put it into the bowl. From the table he grabbed a lighter. "I can't tell you how good it makes me feel," he said. He flicked the lighter, which blew a torch-like flame into the bowl, and he sucked. The hit took longer than I expected, at least a half-minute. He pulled the bong away from his face, exhaling. I couldn't see the smoke. "Here, take a hit," he said. He angled the bong towards me.

"No," I said, almost jumping backwards. My tone revealed more than I'd intended. It told Lance, in the unspoken language of childhood friends, that I wanted no part of this new habit of his. It also said—as unmistakably as if I'd yelled it at him—that this is the point at which we diverge. He was going his way with drugs, and I was going my way with the band, even though the other members meant nothing to me compared to him. I knew this drug habit, sooner or later, would force the others to make a move on him, and I would side with them when they did.

Lance pulled himself up against the headrest, stared at the TV.

"You going out with us tonight?" I asked. "The A&R guys promised a fancy dinner."

"I might be down," Lance said. He didn't take his eyes off the TV.

* * *

Buzzing back to San Paolo in the blue something-or-other, Pippy asks, "Were any of your bandmates into drugs?"

She saw the band the night I flaked on them. She must be throwing the members around, trying to find the problem. "We all had our moments," I say.

"Even you?" she says, surprised.

"Even me," I say.

"Joshua Hotle engaged in such unhealthy activities as drugs and alcohol?"

"I was quite the drinker in my day."

"Ha!" she says. She slaps the steering wheel. "Hote, the rock 'n' roll rebel. Grow out your hair a little and you could be in Mott the Hoople."

"Hey," I say, perturbed that I come across as so tame. "I rocked big time. Trust me."

"You *do* rock big time," she says. She leers at me as she turns up Main Street.

Gad

Listen. Hote's a good kid, a great bass player, but we know what this is about, don't we?

I've dealt with it my whole life. As I got shuffled from town to town, school to school, it was always the same. The new kid shows up, the girls go crazy, and the boys—the ones who've never been anywhere in their lives—start plotting their revenge. It made it hard, I admit it, but it taught me how to deal with all kinds.

I could see it coming from Hote a mile away. Those thrift store clothes, the haircut, his glances shot at me every time I spoke. "Say what you want," he seemed to say, "but I'll never trust you." Fine. Don't trust me. I can work with that. Been doing it for years. I certainly didn't need his approval. In fact, I don't need him at all anymore.

I can admit he had something when we started, and I didn't care to venture forth without it. I first noticed it during a Friday night gig at Chuy's, our first packed house. About halfway through the set, the crowd started chanting, a soft, rhythmic thump off to the right. I assumed they were chanting "chug, chug, chug," or some other nonsense, but they weren't. Once I looked down and saw their glasses aloft, I knew they weren't slamming drinks. They were saluting. That's when I heard it. *Hote, Hote, Hote.*

I've spent a fair amount of time trying to figure it out. Sure, the kid had kissability, a rare compliance to the beat, a way of shaking his head that made him come off as sincere. But the music business doesn't need the bells and whistles of sincerity. It needs a call-to-arms from someone who gets people's attention. Big media—television, radio, press—doesn't care about the band. People hear the song on the radio and they think of one person. Guess who?

So, I bided my time. We would get signed, make a record, play all over the country, and this local stuff would be forgotten. There was something coming down the pipe that he couldn't control, and it would slant the court in my favor.

But it didn't happen quickly enough. We had nibbles, about the same as Jejune July, but no one wanted to make the commitment. Our trip to South-by-Southwest yielded *nada*, and it was back to Tempe, where the crowd still chanted his name.

Lance had always been a problem. He was the one guy who talked back, who didn't take direction. He questioned my songs, challenged them, claimed they could be better than they were. "That bridge isn't right," he'd say, or "The tempo should be faster," or "What are you writing about, anyway?" He even had the balls to suggest we play some of Hote's songs.

"I'm going to ask Lance to leave the band," I announced at practice. The three of us were, as usual, waiting for Lance to show up.

"Oh, really?" Hote said. He laughed, went back to playing his bass guitar, a chordal lick that sounded like something off of a Cure record. Bass players, always struggling to get noticed.

"He shows up late," I said. "He's karmicly out of line with the rest of us. His playing is sloppy."

"He's not sloppy," Hote said. "That's called groove, Gad."

"I know what groove is. There's groove and there's sloppy. Lance is sloppy."

"You should try being sloppy some time," Hote said.

So, I bided my time. I figured it wouldn't be long before Lance screwed it up for himself, and it wasn't.

I first found out about Lance's crystal habit when Denise, his on-again, off-again girlfriend, stopped by my apartment. Cute girl. Tennis outfit, tan legs, little blonde ponytail. Too bad I'm holding out for someone with more leverage.

She told me she was breaking up with Lance, "for good this time," and she wanted me to know why. "There are drugs involved," she said. She didn't know what kind—and he got furious when she asked about it—but she'd overheard him talking on the phone about something called "meth." "I thought you guys might be able to help him," she said.

"Of course," I said. "You did the right thing. We'll make sure Lance gets all the help he needs."

"That's it," I announced at our next practice. "He's out. We can't afford that kind of baggage." We were playing showcases around the country, and Amythyst was talking numbers and contract duration. Lance's little problem threatened everything.

"It's his ex-girlfriend," Hote said. "Don't you think she has her own agenda?"

"You've seen the way he's been acting," I said.

Even Hote couldn't deny it. The distance, the edginess, Lance's removal of himself from all non-gig activity. Hote knew what I knew. Lance would kill it for us.

I came to rehearsal one day and heard yelling from inside the practice room. It sounded like Hote and Lance, but I couldn't make out the words. I tried to slip in discreetly, but they heard me.

"What's all the ruckus?" I asked.

Neither spoke.

"Come on, boys," I said. "Enough with the secrets. What are you two fighting about?"

"None of your business," Hote said.

"Oh, but it is my business if my bandmates aren't getting along. Let's see. What could it be? A dispute over bass drum patterns?"

There's a moment when the cosmic power of a band tilts, when the politics shift just enough for you to take advantage and run with it. That's when a band goes from its local to its national identity, from pub band to arena band, from diversion to destiny. I know right when that happened for Fun Yung Moon.

It was a month before we got signed. The three of us, Hote, Verge and I, lingered in the parking lot of the Boom Boom Café on Mill Avenue. We'd just met with Mitchell Lowenstein, who would become our business manager. Nothing was said, by Mitch or by us, about the fact that Lance hadn't shown up for the meeting. It was the most recent of a few he'd missed, and it would be his last.

We always got together after these meetings to discuss the candidate. Despite how little we got along, our votes on who would make up our team were surprisingly unanimous. Glen and Eli Gathwaight, our lawyer, both made the cut without dissent. Mitch, we decided, would work fine, but that wasn't the last of our business that day.

"So," I said. "Anyone know where Lance is?"

Hote sat on the tailgate of his pickup truck, stared down at his shoes. "I have no idea," he said.

"Did he call?"

"Didn't call me."

Traffic puttered by on Mill Avenue. I stared at Hote, waiting for him to stage some kind of defense of his friend, but he said nothing.

"Well," I said. "That's three in a row he's skipped out on. What are we gonna do about it?"

No one said anything. Verge, as usual, hid behind a cloud of cigarette smoke, waiting for someone else to make a decision he could go along with. Hote wouldn't look up.

"Any suggestions?" I said.

"Let's throw him out," Hote said.

And there it was, the cosmic turn of events that would send us into orbit. I was completely for it, of course, but I didn't think it would come that easily. Hote was serving it up to me. "Well," I said. "There's an idea. Verge, how do you feel about it?"

Verge sucked on his cigarette, looked up at the sky. "Lance gets the best marijuana I've ever smoked," he said, "but that only counts for so much. If everyone else wants him out, it's all right with me."

"Okay," I said. "There's one. I'm for it. There's two. That leaves you, Hote. You brought it up, but it only seems fair to ask you again. We're prepared to kick Lance out of the band. Are you?"

He sat on his tailgate, not looking up from his shoes. After a moment, he hopped to his feet and slammed the tailgate shut. "Let's get it over with," he said. "If it were me, I'd want to know quick."

I don't think Hote ever recovered from that. His playing suffered; trying to lock with another drummer confused him. He looked ridiculous onstage, a strange disconnect that kept him back by his amp most of the time. He faked it sometimes, but any thirteen-year-old could see right through him. We signed with Amythyst that summer, and I've never looked back.

So, now he blames me, of course, making a scene in front of the band, running out on all of us. I always thought he was a little too sensitive for this game. He, of course, is free of my tyranny from here on out, but it won't be long before he finds the tyranny of the world a much greater nemesis. He'll go run some other race, and he'll look back one day and realize that without Fun Yung Moon there is no race, and that his problems had nothing whatever to do with me.

* * *

Someone knocks on the bus door.

I can't deal with Fresno riff-raff right now. The bus was supposed to be a quiet place to practice my mantra. Nothing's going as planned these days. I'll be lucky to get ten minutes in before the gig.

I peek out the tinted windows. It's just one guy. He doesn't look like a fan, at least forty-five, sketchy features, T-shirt and jeans. I'd like to ignore him, but he doesn't look like he's going away anytime soon. I flip open the bus door. "Can I help you?" I say.

"Josh here?"

"Who?"

"Josh," he says. "He's a guy in the band."

"I'm sorry. There's no Josh in the band. You've got the wrong bus."

The man looks over his shoulder, at the people milling about the gate. "You're Fun Yung Moon, right? The guy at the front said this is Fun Yung Moon's bus."

"Yeah, but Fun Yung Moon has no Josh."

"Oh, yeah," the guy says. He grimaces. "How 'bout Hote? Is Hote here?"

"What do you know about Hote?" I say. I step out onto the sidewalk. "Did he tell you he was coming?"

"No," the guy says. "I just knew the band was gonna be here and–"

"Well, we haven't seen Hote since Orange County," I say, "and we probably never will again. He's out of the band."

"Out of the band?" the guy says.

"He ran out on us in San Paolo. Nobody's seen him, and nobody wants to."

"Oh," the guy says. He scratches his head. "Why'd he do that?"

"You know what?" I say. I'm not wasting my whole day with this cretin. It's a big world. He can get his info someplace else. "I really don't care." I turn to get back on the bus, but I feel his hand grab my shoulder.

"Hey," I say and spin around.

"You shouldn't turn your back on people when they're talking to you," he says.

"What?"

"I'm talking to you," he says, "and you turned your back on me. That can lead to trouble."

"Are you threatening me?"

The guy takes out a cigarette and puts it in his mouth. "No," he says. He lights it. "Just talking."

"You wanna talk?" I say. "Okay. Let's talk. Hote got the best treatment he could've ever hoped for from this band, and what does he do? What does that little prick do the first time he doesn't get exactly what he wants? He strands us without a bass player with a thousand people waiting. I've been looking for a word that sums up how pissed off I am at him, but I can't find one. None of them are harsh enough."

The guy squints at me, blows smoke out his mouth. He looks calm, but something in the glaze of his eyes suggests more. "Where's the last place you saw him?" he says.

"I don't have to answer you," I say and turn towards the door.

The guy rushes me. I scramble back onto the bus and go to shut the door, but he wedges his body in before I can close it. I stumble up the stairs, knocking my incense onto the floor, and he comes after me, forcing me backwards onto my ass. He plants his forearm under my chin and pushes my head against the couch. I don't dare move. He stares at me, his eyes round bulbs.

"Where's the last place you saw him?" he says.

"The Equinox, San Paolo."

"How long ago?"

"Yesterday."

He lets his arm off my throat and stands up. He looks down at me, puffs air out his nose. Then he smiles, a big smile that would scare even his mother. He shuffles down the stairs and slams the door behind him.

I get up and go to the front window, watch him run up the sidewalk and around the corner. *Nobody saw.* I rub my neck. *Nobody saw, so it never happened.* I lock the bus door.

No Reservations

"Thanks for having me to dinner," I say, nodding at Alex and Gloria Koenig. The table's set for the four of us. Pippy's next to me. Gloria, Pippy's mom, in a clingy black sweat suit, sits at one end. Alex, Pippy's dad, a large, balding man in a white business shirt, sits at the other. A cardboard box from Pizza Chief is open in the middle of the table. I've been invited to dinner on the assumption that I'm Pippy's new boyfriend. I almost hit her when she said that. "Don't you think they'll be a little concerned about my age?" I said. "Don't worry," Pippy said, grabbing my hand. "I always date older guys. Anyway, you could pass for college if you wanted."

"So, Hote," Gloria says. The light from the chandelier gives the room a mellow, tinted glow. Everything feels too formal. I'm devouring my pizza; I want this meal over with as soon as possible. "How did you meet Betty, anyway? She didn't drag you here from that concert last night, did she?"

It takes a moment for me to realize she's talking about Pippy. *Betty.* I can see the Betty in her, the soft, conventional side she's so intent on hiding. "Actually, yes," I say, liking that it's almost the truth. "We went bowling today. Your daughter's quite a bowler."

"Ah, yes," Gloria says. She pulls her legs up underneath her. Her black ninja shoes make her feet look tiny. "We'd hoped she'd go pro. Then, rock 'n' roll came along." She wipes her hands on her napkin, even though she has yet to touch her pizza.

"Actually, it was the meth that pushed me over the edge," Pippy says.

"Crystal meth," Alex says, loud enough to startle me. The light from the chandelier reflects off his glasses, which sit far down his nose. What's left of his short, dark hair is peppered gray. Despite all this, he seems playful, a corporate guy refusing to live a corporate life at home. "Kids these days. They used to call it speed, or—what did they call it when you shot up speed?"

"Freebasing," Pippy says. She reaches for another slice of pizza.

"No," Alex says. "I'm talking about shooting up speed." He snaps his fingers, then pushes them into his forearm, syringe-like. "There's a name for it."

"I'm not sure this is appropriate dinner conversation," Gloria says.

"Speed-balling," Alex says, surprising himself. "They called it speed-balling back in the day. That's what Sid and Nancy died from."

"That was heroin," Pippy says. She picks a piece of cheese from the box and pops it in her mouth.

Alex sets down his pizza. He swears he knows this. "Hote, tell Betty what Sid and Nancy died from."

"I'm pretty sure it was heroin," I say.

"Agh," Alex says. He wipes the conversation away with his hand. "What do you two know about shootin' smack? Nothing, that's what."

The stereo plays what the DJ calls "smooth jazz" but what actually sounds like bland pop.

"Hote," Gloria says. She has a smart, questioning way about her, and she seems likely to ask the right question, which scares me. "Where are you from?"

"Phoenix," I say. "My mom lives in Ahwatukee."

"Oh," Gloria says. "So you came all this way for the show?"

"You could say that."

"Oh, yeah. I almost forgot," Pippy says. She sets her pizza down and glances at both of her parents. "Mom, Dad, can Hote crash in the rec room tonight? He's got nowhere to stay, and I don't want him to leave for Phoenix just yet."

"I don't know," Gloria says. "Hote, will your mother miss you?"

"Um, no," I say. "I'm old enough to pretty much call my own shots that way."

"Well," Gloria says. "I guess I have no objections to Hote sleeping *downstairs, by himself,* for one night. Alex, do you mind?"

Alex takes another bite of pizza, contemplating. "Absolutely no spliff smokin' in this house," he says, pounding his fist on the table.

* * *

I didn't realize it for a long time, but most of the great art of the world was created by assholes.

Celia first pointed it out to me. We were at her apartment during the semester I went back to college, where we spent most of our time "studying." Celia, wearing nothing but my Prior Angels T-shirt, warmed up leftovers in the kitchen. We were cramming for finals, the World War II novelists, Mailer, Heller, Kurt Vonnegut. She took notes from their biographies, and I outlined the works.

"Mailer's an ass," Celia said. She pushed chicken around in a saucepan. I loved the way she looked, the tan lines around her ankles, her legs the color of butterscotch ice cream. "He had seven wives. Stabbed one of them! What a nut job."

"What alimony he must pay," I said. We'd just made love, and I was experiencing a large dose of after-sex antagonism. We both recognize this tendency in me. Celia thinks it's natural, that I'm frustrated because I can't get away after my biological duty's been performed. I, of course, disagree with her, but I can disagree with anything at these times.

"And he deserves every bit of it," she said.

"Elizabeth Taylor had eight husbands. I wonder if she pays alimony."

"My god," Celia said. She ran her hand through her pleasantly messed-up blond hair. "I can't believe you're defending this guy."

"I'm not defending him," I said. "He's probably a complete jerk, but anyone who writes *The Naked and the Dead* gets a little leeway in my book."

"So you think the art justifies the life," she said. "You think someone can be the biggest asshole on the planet as long as he delivers the goods."

"I don't think anyone has the right to be an asshole," I said, "but looking back at someone's life you have to consider whether that person did something truly great. Would we dismiss Picasso because he turned out to be a lousy husband to his wife?"

"Wives," Celia said, smiling.

"You know what I mean," I said.

"I'm not disqualifying anything," she said. "*The Naked and the Dead* rules, but it's hard for me to read those bios without wondering what kind of husbands these guys were to their wives, especially when they had seven of them."

"And stabbed one of them," I said, getting up and heading for the kitchen.

"Stay away from the knife set," Celia said.

* * *

We're in Pippy's bedroom. Alex and Gloria watch TV in the den, something loud that echoes through the house. I stand next to the open bedroom door, where Gloria can walk by any time she wants and see that Pippy and I are having nothing but a thoroughly decent evening together, even though I've mentally undressed her daughter a few times since dinner.

"Damn idiot box," Pippy says. She slams the door and, not quite accidentally, brushes up against me.

"Don't like TV?" I ask. I flip through her CD collection, surprised to find artists I like, Pavement, the Specials, Minor Threat.

"I think we should destroy every one of them," she says.

"That's a bold statement," I say. "You never watch TV?"

"Not unless I'm forced to," she says. She's changed clothes again—the third time today—from her skirt outfit into a white, clingy top with straps over her shoulders, and brown, UPS-style pants. She grabs a copy of *Alternative Press* and opens it. "You only get fluff on MTV. I hate the fluff more than I hate anything."

"Just so we fully understand each other," I say. "What's 'the fluff'?"

"Oh, come on," she says. "Everyone knows what the fluff is. You see it, and you know it." Her eyes brighten. She's found something in the magazine. "Take a look at this."

It's a picture of Fun Yung Moon from our last photo shoot, a shot taken in the desert outside Phoenix. Gad's up front, his face pushed into the camera. The rest of us are behind him. I wear Elvis-style sunglasses that are supposed to make me look cool but instead make me look like an accountant on a weekend fling.

"Don't show me that," I say.

"Why'd you do it?" she asks.

"It was either the sunglasses or a cowboy hat. I saw it as the lesser of two evils."

"The lesser of two evils is inherently evil."

"Thanks, Pippy," I say. "Thanks for clarifying that."

"I just don't understand it." She slides on her belly to the edge of the bed. Her top scoots down, revealing her cleavage. "You're a free agent. You don't need them. Why would you allow them to push you into something you don't want to do? Is it the money?"

"No," I say.

"The fame?"

"Hell, no."

"Then what?"

It's a good question. There was a time, a moment almost, when I wanted the band to succeed more than anything. I had a belief that people *needed* to hear Fun Yung Moon, that we could entertain, inform, maybe even instruct in a weird way. Why did I think that? Why did I believe that what we were doing was not only good but important, so much so that it led to me looking silly in national magazines? "I guess I loved it, Pip," I say. "I loved it in a way you probably shouldn't love a band."

"Oh," Pippy says. She rolls her eyes, goes back to her magazine.

"You know," I say. In her CDs I find a copy of Hüsker Dü's *Warehouse: Songs and Stories*. It's a favorite of mine from high school. I haven't heard it in ages. I pull it out. "Like you care about something so much you'd do almost anything for it." I find the CD player on her stereo and pop it in.

"Yes," Pippy says. "I've heard of love. Never really believed in it, though."

"What?" I say. "Pippy doesn't believe in love?"

"That's about it."

"Well, I'm still holding out hope for you."

"Don't bother," she says. "You should see those two go at it when you're not here." She points with her head towards the door, her parents.

The first song of the CD, "These Important Years," comes through the stereo. The tone of the music, shrill, almost desperate, jolts me to the point that I'm a little scared of it. It's funny how nothing since its release, even post-Nirvana, can give me the jitters like Hüsker Dü. "My folks didn't get along, either," I say, "but I don't think it has to be that way."

"You think it can work?"

Despite all evidence to the contrary—my mom and dad splitting up; Celia sleeping around on me; me, a married man, hanging out with a high school girl in her bedroom—I say, "I don't see why not."

"How 'bout that it's never worked for anyone in the history of the planet?" she says. "Is that a good enough reason?"

"Maybe," I say. "But you might be stretching it just a bit."

"Whatever," she says. "Hit the 'next' button, would you? This song skips."

* * *

I do believe in love. I believe in bold, faith-based declarations to one other person. I believe in patient, un-paranoid sex with someone you'll never quite understand. I believe, as William Faulkner said, in the soul and the glands, and the difference between the two. One screams for attention, the other whispers whole books without ever getting boring. One moves closer, the other is always a breath away. One is worth it for the moment, the other colors every moment for the rest of your life.

Celia and I used to carry that love with us everywhere. Where did it go? Where is mine now?

* * *

"Thanks for letting me crash here," I say.

Pippy and I are in the hallway just outside of her bedroom. Pictures of her extended family, cousins from other states, sepias of dead ancestors, line the walls. A blanket and pillow sit on a wooden chair, my bedding laid out by Gloria. Hüsker Dü's "No Reservations" comes faintly into the hallway from her bedroom. The TV still echoes from downstairs.

"No problem," she says. She looks up at me, arms crossed, eyes glistening. "Anything I can do for a rock star in need."

"Cool," I say.

She slides closer, a sideways move that brings her thigh into contact with mine. "I may be down later," she whispers. She eases her hand over my stomach. "After everyone's asleep."

I sense her below me, her bare stomach, her long neck. She seems small enough to eat in one bite, and this fact alone makes me want to swallow her. "You probably shouldn't," I say.

"The best reason there is," she says.

Alex

"You need to watch them," Gloria says. "They're kids. They won't watch themselves."

It pulls me away from *The Next Generation*. The space between Gloria's eyes forms a little X, which makes her look like one of the aliens on the show. I know that look. It means, *Pay attention. You can't screw this up and laugh it off later.*

"They're old enough to take care of themselves," I say. "That kid looks about twenty-five to me."

"Exactly," she says. "Are you going to leave your daughter alone with a twenty-five-year-old?"

"We let her date him," I say. "I don't know how we can watch them every min–"

"We can watch them while they're here," she says. The X goes boldface.

Gloria goes to bed, and I stay up to watch them. I look Hote over when he comes downstairs, even though I don't need to. I know what this kid wants. What does every kid want? I know it without ever looking at him.

He walks past the living room on his way to the basement, carrying the blankets. It's the same way my assistant walks into the office Monday morning after calling in sick on Friday. "Feeling better?" I always ask her. If I don't, I'm an insensitive bastard, right? But it always sounds like I'm needling her. "Yeah," she says. "I think it passed." The company gives her ten sick-days a year. I think she should take them.

"Thanks again for letting me sleep here," he says, and he tries to keep going.

"Hote," I say. I turn off the TV. "Come in here a second."

He looks at me like a squirrel at an approaching car; he wants to run, but he's not sure which direction to go. He comes into the living room and sits on the couch, not sitting back.

I rub my hand over my eyes, pop my lips together. "Say, I'm thirsty. You wanna beer?"

"Not really," he says. "I've got a big trip ahead of me tomorrow."

I grunt my way out of the recliner. "You sure?"

"Yeah."

"Suit yourself." I walk to the kitchen. This is the way, back when I was growing up, girls' fathers used to do it. You get the kid comfortable, get him a drink, then scare the shit out of him. At some point, he'll be alone with my daughter. When he is, I want him thinking of me. I grab a beer from the fridge and pop the top. "Last chance," I call into the living room.

"No, thanks," he says.

The kid's not a drinker. One strike against him already.

I come back and he's looking at the framed pictures along the wall. "Is that Jerry Garcia?" he asks.

It's the small, faded snapshot of me with the Dead in sixty-eight. I'm wearing a yellow Cozumel T-shirt over my skinny frame. My arms are around both Phil Lesh and Bob Weir. Garcia's way over to the right, but he's the only one anyone ever recognizes. "That was a long time ago," I said.

"You met him?"

"I met the whole band in Santa Cruz."

"No way," he says. "What were they like?"

I shrug my shoulders. "Like anybody. Bob was worried about

getting something to eat. Phil has this snooty voice. You'd think he was a professor or something. Now, Jerry—" I get a little choked up mentioning his name. Funny, because I didn't even cry when he died. Hot morning two months ago, driving up 101 to work, listening to the news on the radio. Too busy, I guess. "Jerry was something special."

"I'm so envious of that time," he says.

You should be. Tangy and I were going to drop out of school, buy a van, follow them forever. "Why?" I ask, just to see if he gets it.

"It seems so ideal," he says. "There was so much possibility for what could be, and it all came from the love of music."

"Among other things," I say. I set my beer down. "You know what we did the night of that concert? Tangy and me—Tangy's the second guy from the left—we bought ten hits of speed and ten hits of acid and—" I stop myself. Twenty-five years old or not, this is Betty's boyfriend. "I shouldn't be telling you this."

"It's okay," he says. "I'd really like to know. I won't tell anyone."

I smile. Brown hair, round face, this kid kinda looks like Tangy. "We took all the drugs and dropped them into a bottle filled with water. 'Electric wine,' we called it. I was so fried I don't even remember the show." I laugh. Sometimes I wonder how I survived it all.

"What happened to Tangy?" he asks.

"I don't know," I say. "He probably bought a VW bus and lived the dream for both of us. He didn't show up to school the next semester, I know that."

"You think he's still out there?"

I see bums around all the time—dirty tie-dyes, sitting like broken stickmen against buildings—and I wonder if it's him. I'm not sure I'd recognize him. "Somewhere," I say. "Listen, we boomers, we talk about the sixties like it was some paradise, but it was just our youth. You guys, Betty, you have your own youth. You shouldn't be too wrapped up in ours."

"You guys had more than youth," he says. "You had a cause. You could bum around all day or go on road trips or get messed up on the craziest shit ever, and it was all okay because it was for the right cause. We don't have that anymore. If I bum around, I'm just lazy. If I do drugs, I'm just killing brain cells."

"Wanna see something?" I say. The kid wants to know about the sixties? I've got something for him. I scoot behind the television and unhook the latch of the cabinet that never gets opened. I reach in, all the way to the side where Betty could never find it, and feel the long steel piping of Old Faithful. I pull it out.

"It's a bong," he says.

"Old Faithful," I say. I run my hand up the piping, brush dust off the maple base. "Gloria only let me keep it after I promised never to let Betty know about it, so keep this under your hat."

The kid takes the bong and holds it in both hands, kind of at an angle, like he's posing with a trophy fish. "Why 'Old Faithful'?" he asks.

"The guys on my dorm floor called it that because it was guaranteed to go off every hour for the whole semester. You see, you put water in it." I can't stand the way he's holding it. I take it from him. "Come in here."

I lead him to the kitchen, angle the bong under the faucet. "The smoke filters through the water and makes for a smooth hit." I take the bong and put it to my mouth. My suck makes bubbles. I lift my thumb off the carburetor and inhale. "That's all there is to it."

"Can I try it?" he asks.

"There's nothing in it," I say. "I scraped all the resin out years ago."

"I know," he says. "I just want to see how it hits."

I give him the bong and he puts it to his mouth. He looks down and sucks. The water rattles too much in the chamber.

"The key is the carburetor," I say. I show him the hole. "Put your thumb over it. That's what fills the pipe with smoke."

The kid sucks and makes the bubbles rattle.

"Then, when it's ready, you take your thumb off."

He does, and pretends to hold the hit in his mouth. He blows it out with an exaggerated puff. "That's the best Acapulco Gold I've ever had," he says.

I take the bong, try a hit. "That's some kind bud," I say. "Where'd you score it?"

"Big Manny up the street," he says, and we both laugh.

"What the hell's going on in here?"

It's Gloria. Her hair's not tied back, and all of her make-up is off. She wears her blue kimono, an acknowledgement that there's company in the house and we can't parade around in our underwear. "I, um—Hote was asking about the sixties and—"

"And you decided to reefer-up in the kitchen."

"There's nothing in it," I say. I show her the bong. "We haven't even lit it. I was just giving Hote a little history lesson."

"That's the truth," Hote says. "I was just heading down to the basement and—"

"Maybe you should head down now," Gloria says.

"No problem," he says and ducks out, leaving me to deal with the fallout.

I hate this, Gloria pinning me in for some wrong I've brought upon the family or whatever. Hey, I've supported keeping Betty away from drugs. It's exactly the right thing to do. If the girl gets into drugs, it won't be because she learned it at home. But there's reality, too. There's the fact that it's out there, that it's fascinating, that at some point Betty's gonna get offered it—if she hasn't been already— and do we want to wait until afterwards to address it? It doesn't have to be a hard conversion. Yes, honey, we tried drugs, and while we may not regret every minute of being on them, they pale in comparison to being lucid and cognizant and fully within your faculties. Drugs are what I did before you and your mother came into my life. Drugs are a consolation prize for losing out on happiness.

Gloria paces the kitchen, her arms crossed. She looks small in her kimono, a Japanese housewife contemplating bad news, weighing the shame brought upon the family name. "I thought we had a deal," she says.

"We did," I say. "We do. The kid got me going on the Dead and I got carried away."

"You think he's not gonna tell her about this?" she says. Her face is somehow crueler without make-up. "It's her boyfriend."

"I don't know how long that's gonna last," I say. "He's going home tomorrow."

"And until then?" she says. "They'll have a great time chatting about Daddy's bong in the morning."

"Hote won't say anything. He wasn't as impressed as you might think. Kids today, drugs don't hold the same sway over them as they did with us."

"Right," she says, incredulous. "And that Cobain guy killed himself because he couldn't find a good parking space or something."

"Actually, Cobain was quite sick. There's a theory that it wasn't drugs so much as—"

"I don't care," Gloria says. She's crying now. The tears stew in her eyes, and I know I've lost. I can't stand it when she cries. I'll concede anything. "I don't care why some drugged out musician killed himself. I don't want our daughter to become a drugged out musician. That's it. The rest of rock 'n' roll can go jump in a lake."

I take her in my arms, feel this prim, kimonoed woman under my hands. "It won't happen," I say. "We won't let it."

* * *

I put the bong away, and Gloria heads upstairs. I try to follow her.

"Whoa," she says. "Where do you think you're going?"

"To bed."

"Sorry," she says. "You're still on duty."

"What? The kids are asleep."

She looks at me like I must be the most naive guy who ever lived. "Don't you remember anything about being sixteen?" she says, and she disappears up the stairs.

I fall into the recliner, grab the remote control. *Star Trek*'s over. Now *Friends* is on. I never understood the attraction to this show. They play up all the female characters at the expense of the men. There's the puppy-love guy, the guy you never quite believe Aniston would go for. There's the neurotic guy, who'd be funnier if he had a real male presence to play off of. There's the completely harmless sex maniac. All three are as benign as Shredded Wheat.

The girls are nice to look at, though. Big boobs, hippy clothes, Miss Clairol hair. I never understood why Betty didn't go for it.

"It's the way they want you to look," she said.

"Who are 'they'?" I said.

"Corporate America," she said. "It's all a ruse to get everyone to be a certain way. That's how they control you."

"It's a TV show," I said. "Its job is to *entertain* you," but she pretended not to hear.

I take a tug of my beer, which has gotten warm. I'm tired and I want to go to bed, but apparently I'm supposed to stay up all night to make sure nothing happens. Why do I have to stay up? I'm the one who has work tomorrow.

I toss down the rest of the beer and go get another. If I'm stuck watching TV by myself I can at least make it interesting. I break off one more from the six-pack and pop the top. Maybe I can find some old movie. *Cool Hand Luke* plays every week or so on cable. I might get lucky.

Those girls on *Friends* are wonderful. There's something about their shapes that makes them perfect for TV. It's like, if you saw them in real life, you wouldn't think that much of them, but on TV they're goddesses. They found their medium.

I flop back into my chair, take another tug. I wonder if I ever found my medium. When I was a kid, my parents tried to get me to take piano. Scales, chords, "Chopsticks," I didn't have the patience for it. Too bad. I could've been a decent musician, maybe even better than that. Guess we'll never know.

I take a tug of my beer, wipe my lips. *Friends* is over. We've moved on to some sit-com I've never bothered to learn the name of. I click the TV off. Betty's right. The thing sucks you in.

The good old days—I guess that's what you'd call them, but it doesn't sound right. Andy Griffith, fishing poles and minnow buckets, my good old days have nothing to do with that. My good old days are bad old days for people who love good old days. Tangy and the bong, watching the Dead through acid lenses, screwing whoever whenever. I loved it so much I almost gave up everything for it. Sometimes I wonder if I made the right decision.

I tilt the beer, take a long tug. The quiet's nice, like the time Gloria and I went to Mexico. A shack on the beach, the ocean lapping the shore, calypso music. I always loved calypso music, the sound of the steel drums synching in and out with the waves. We sat on the beach and drank. Pineapple. The drink had pineapple and something else. Rum? I don't know. I can't remember, but I remember the taste. I can still taste it.

We listened to calypso music and drank. The taste of the pineapple and rum in my mouth *Do you want to try something different?* My face under her long hair, her hair long back then. The calypso music was all around us. We danced close up, her ass against me, my hands on her hips at the top of her skirt. *Like what?* I loved her for that. Earrings jangling like flowers in the wind like motion like mangos falling from the trees.

Right out on the street. Nothing could touch the magic of the street. *I want you here. I want you with the moonlight and the mangos and the people walking by.* Can there be anything like the summer and the heat and the moonlight, the motion and the smell of mango in the street? I tasted the rum on her neck and the calypso. I tasted the salt on her throat and the waves in the ocean. Could she ever use those words again . . . *Like what?* . . . like the words . . . the night and the breath and the tongue . . . the mangos in the ocean . . . the words . . . I can't remember . . . I can't

Rec Room

A ping-pong table, unplayed for years, takes up most of the space down here. A couch, beanbag chair and TV are stashed in the smaller part where I've bedded down. It looks like Pippy tried to make this into a jam room at one point; guitar magazines are all over the place, and pages of chord configurations are taped to the wall. An acoustic guitar leans in one corner, collecting dust. The heat vent blows down on me. I barely need a blanket.

The couch reminds me of the couch in our living room when I was growing up, the couch I shared with dates in high school. We'd rent videos or watch a movie on HBO, huddled together under a blanket. The trick was to get their attention off the movie and onto me. When I found someone willing, a trap door opened inside of me, flooding me with urgency. I'd relinquish anything; love, marriage, a pound of flesh, all valuables were considered.

The basement door opens and closes. It's Pippy. Her presence seems too sudden. It's like the events leading up to this moment happened somewhere outside of me, when I was only half thinking. I turn the table lamp off and lie still on the couch, hoping she'll think I'm asleep. The thumps of her feet come down the stairs.

"Pip," I say into the darkness. It's really dark, a dark that only follows the turning out of a light. Pippy doesn't answer, but I hear her stop on the stairs.

"Don't come down here," I say.

I hear nothing. She must be standing there, trying to gauge my motive. I can picture her, hands on both rails, each foot frozen on a different stair.

"Why not?" she says, a whisper unlike any voice I've heard from her. Its closest companion is her singing voice, soft, vulnerable.

"Because I don't want you to," I say.

"Why?"

"Go to bed."

I hear the footsteps continue down the stairs. I don't see her come around the corner, but I can sense her in the room, the sound of her breath, her body giving the darkness life.

"If it's my age," she says. "I wouldn't let it bother you. It doesn't bother me."

"Pip," I say. "I'm married."

She stops at the couch. The slight creak of her presence hovers above me. "How come you never mentioned it before?"

"I don't know," I say. "I didn't think it was important before."

I can make her out now. Her head, a silhouette, looks down on me. She wears some kind of robe tied at the waist, the hem coming to the middle of her thighs. She reaches down, touches my hand. "Do you love her?"

Her touch reminds me, strangely enough, of Celia, the loving touch of Celia. It feels wrong to think of her now, but in another way it feels exactly right, like I'm missing her, missing the love we used to give to each other. I want that now more than anything.

I interlock my hand with Pippy's and guide her down to the couch.

The difference between Celia and Pippy shocks me. Pippy's body has little give, her muscles young and tight. Celia is soft, pliant; one squeeze and I know why I love her. But I still feel Celia through Pippy, the outline of her waist, the wet lips against mine, perfume. My body vibrates. I'm thrilled that the world of other women still has something to offer me.

Pippy unzips my pants and fumbles in my underwear. A rough, sudden shifting and my cock is out, encircled by her hand. She pumps awkwardly, like she's playing with a joystick of a video game she has yet to master. "Easy," I say, and I stop her, wrap her fingers in mine.

Lovemaking is the search for space. The thumbprint under the pelvis, the divot of the collarbone, the bump in the throat. I explore every crevice, and I get charged by the rushes they give me. I can tell Pippy gets no equal thrill from it, that her motions are somewhat forced, that the charm only works in one direction. It dawns on me that she doesn't really want me, in the way Celia or some other girl might want me. Pippy is more of a gift to me, a gift from Betty to me. *A gift for what?* For information? For friendship? For being one notch above her on some ladder of fame? I don't know. I don't want to know. It can only make me stop. When I slide into her, I drink in Pippy's breath and feel her legs wrap around me like wings.

* * *

Right afterwards, she's off me.

She stands next to the couch, her silhouette searching the floor for her robe. "Listen," she says. "I gotta go."

"When did you get up?"

"I'm sorry," she says. She finds her robe and puts it on. "I shouldn't have done this."

"Don't be sorry," I say. I reach for her. "You don't have to run off."

"Yes, I do," she says.

"Why?" I say, but I know why. Without the urgency of needing her, the chemistry in the room—the way the darkness looks, the smell of the air—has changed. It's clear that this didn't have to happen, that it was all just flashing lights that dim, that it was a moment, and like all moments it ticked away, leaving nothing but its residue. "I'm sorry," I say.

"There's a shower in the laundry room if you need it," Pippy says. I hear her climb up the stairs, leaving me alone for the night.

Friday

Celia

It's a hard thing to give up, the Impulse, that is. I've tried to give it up for years now. Sometimes I'm successful, sometimes less so. But no matter where or when or how I slip off with the Impulse, I always come back. I know where home is, what I lack and don't lack, what comes naturally and what I have to work on.

This whole world wants to keep going as is. Video games, money, the soft curves of plastic toddler toys. There's nothing to it but the Impulse. From the outside, nobody ever finds the facts. Nobody ever works the edges into curves the way I work with words, all day, fighting them into cohesion. No one ever books the flights or fights the traffic or cleans the cabanas. To them, it's all just one big Fantasy Island.

They bring their poker faces to work, play at being busy. Eyes up, quick nod. Still, come deadline time they're scrambling to get it together, and you know all week wasn't spent working. They were seduced by the Impulse. It's okay. I've been seduced by it, too. It happens to everyone.

The first time I saw Josh play I knew, *I'm marrying that man. Ten kids. Wait and see.* Oh, we'd been seeing each other for a week or so by then, but it was seeing him play that made me light on fire for him. He didn't so much play the songs as will his way through them. His foot stomped with the beat, his head bounced. He pushed his pelvis forward when it really took over. The man was present, and I couldn't take my eyes off him. Afterwards it was planned we'd meet backstage, but I wished I'd never met him. I wanted to seduce him in the parking lot to see how far he'd let me go without ever exchanging our names. There was nothing in the world but the pursuit of him, and he was already mine.

"I'm going back to school," he announced. "I'm going to school with you." I told him to quit being foolish—he's a musician—but that didn't keep him from spending his gig money on three classes at A.S.U. I thought, "Great. Now *I'm* responsible for getting him out of bed in the morning." But it wasn't a problem. Josh beat me to the shower, drove us to class, sat and listened to every word out of the instructor's mouth.

The Romantic poets got his attention off the books and onto me. The week of William Blake found us disrobing after class in a sixth-floor bathroom. Josh held me off the ground with the same passion he used to thrust his way through songs. That was heaven, letting him take me to the nearest empty room and consume me with his drive. Once, the rattle of the doorknob sent us scrambling back into our clothes.

But Josh had to quit school when the band got signed, and as much as it broke my heart, I figured it was the best thing for him. He claimed not to want it at all. "Go rock the world," I told him. "It makes sense for a million reasons." But he could tell I was lying, lying right through my teeth to the man I loved. He knew that I thought the band would steal him away from me; that's what bands do. "Think of all the groupies you'll score," I said, but he would have none of it.

"I won't do it," he said. "I won't do it unless you marry me first."

The wedding was simple enough, Little White Chapel in Las Vegas with paid witnesses and no relatives. We buried ourselves in our nuptial bed that whole weekend. He had to be back in Phoenix on Monday so he could fly to Los Angeles, where the band would make its first album, but we got our money's worth. We didn't leave Vegas until we'd lost every penny.

I'm not going to sit here and pretend that I love the band. I can't even say I like them, in the way a fan likes them. If I were stuck on a desert island with no other music but Fun Yung Moon, I can't say I'd prefer them to the sound of the waves crashing, or the call of tropical birds. Still, I played the role of happy wife. It was my job, to support my husband in this thing he cared so much about, even though he seemed to like it less and less all the time. But isn't that life? I wanted to say. Don't we all like things less and less all the time?

At first his transition to the road was seamless. I almost preferred him on the road because he made such an effort to remind me how much he loved me, how much the water in him ebbed and flowed with the thought of me. The postcards, each from a different city, conveyed his torment, the pull between what he had to do and what he needed to do. He had to play these stupid gigs in towns where they'd never heard of Fun Yung Moon: Ames, Omaha, Pig's Knuckle. He needed me, all of me, in any way he could possibly imagine. He needed me more than he needed the Impulse. I *was* his Impulse.

I flew out to surprise him once in New Orleans. I'd just graduated from A.S.U. and wanted to celebrate. The mood on the bus was tense. Even Josh admitted he noticed it. Nobody acknowledged me backstage, or at the hotel, and Josh went out of his way to make me feel appreciated, which only separated him more from the band. "I'm going back home," I told him. I'd planned to tag along up the coast, Florida and the Carolinas, but you couldn't pay me to sleep on the same bus with them. It was worse than work. It was work you had to fake liking, and I'm no good at faking.

The rest, the distance between us when he called from the road, the emotional swings when he was home, our non-existent sex life, all problems that came with the band's success. I told him not to worry about it. "Love fades," I said. "If it's real, that's what it does."

"No," he insisted. "If it's real, it gets more real."

I hung in there with him because he believed it. He believed it enough for both of us.

I went to see him play at Fun Yung Moon's homecoming gig at Mesa Amphitheater. I stood just offstage and watched the kids scream for them. Josh was barely there. He went through these inane motions, going from the front of the stage to the back, back to front, but I couldn't feel him at all. The Impulse, that rotund pull that forced me to love him, had abandoned him, left him alone up there, with all these people watching. I wanted to protect him, to shield him from their looks, but what could I do? Our lives were so separate when he played. If he wanted it, he had to do it himself.

I tried to get him to quit calling every day from the road. The sound of his voice made me too tense, waiting to hear from him only to find him completely out-to-lunch. I got the job at the magazine. There was plenty to keep me busy, but the only way not to wait for his call was not to be expecting one. "Call when you have something to say," I told him. "Don't just call because you have to, because that's what husbands do."

"I have something to say," he said.

"Then say it," I said, but that just made him clam up.

And then he quit calling. I welcomed the silence at first. I could concentrate, impress the boss and pick up slack, but I came to dread the emptiness of life without him. It was too spooky not hearing his voice. I didn't know where he was, what he was doing, what he was thinking. I dreaded coming home at night. I had nobody in Phoenix I could count on; everyone from college had gone their separate ways, and I certainly couldn't tell anyone at work. I needed a stopgap, something easy and comforting and unconnected. I needed to fill the void created by his missing voice.

And I filled it once, only once.

Seth was a custom wood carver who sold his work at the art fair downtown. I stopped by his booth only to grab a card—our boss loves the stuff, has it all over the office—but I quickly got sucked into a conversation about the textures of wood. End tables, bed stands, lamps, he wanted me to touch everything. I nodded and kept listening, or at least I kept watching. He was tall, Italian or something close, with a giant Adam's apple that eased up his throat. There was something rough in his face, a handsome, unadorned roughness, and his interest in his subject—the grain of wood running through a table top, the smell of cedar, the correct amount of sheen to a varnish—made him more handsome. He took every opportunity to touch me. He shook my hand with both of his, held my elbow while showing me around, guided me to avoid people coming into his booth. Nothing forward, but he touched me, triggered flutters inside of me. I could tell I was in the presence of a master of the Impulse. What could I do? A lot, I know now, but back then I thought the Impulse was the top . . . the top of everything. The fair closed down, we had a drink at the hotel bar, and he kissed me in the back booth, where no one could see. When he asked me back to his room, I couldn't say no, couldn't trade it for another night of cigarettes smoked on the back patio by myself.

I came home after midnight to the phone ringing. I knew it was Josh, calling for the first time in who knows how long, but I couldn't make myself answer it. I just sat there on the couch and let it ring. He called again and again, and I cried into my hands, hoping the ringing would stop. He needed me, and there was no way I could be there for him, not after what I'd done. That's when I knew the depth of my failure, knew what I'd given away to the Impulse, and that I would have to tell Josh to get past it.

I remember lying between the sheets in our honeymoon bed, a half-eaten heart of chocolate on the table, each of us needing a shower but not ready to pull ourselves away. "Josh," I said. "What if it doesn't work out?"

He looked at me like I'd said the most confusing thing he'd ever heard. "What?" he said.

"Oh, I don't know," I said. "We could get sick of each other, or we could fall in love with someone else, or the band could pull us apart. All kinds of things could happen."

He turned to me with this stunned look in his eyes that I now recognize as love. "We're married," he said.

And that's the way I approach it now. *We're married.* I could screw up ten—a hundred—times, and we're still married. Josh could have fifty head-banging sluts back to his hotel room, and we're still married. A semi-truck could flatten me on the freeway tomorrow, or the band's bus could drive off a cliff, or god could exact the ultimate penalty on all of us, and even then we're still married. Everything else, even the Impulse, is just a blip on the surface of life.

Riverboat Captain

I didn't sleep well last night. I'd like to say it was because of what happened with Pippy—that would be the right thing to say, the right way to feel—but it had more to do with the song I had stuck in my head. I don't remember ever hearing it before, so I guess I wrote it. I haven't written a song in years. It kept me up until at least two A.M. as I tried to hash it out on the acoustic guitar. The chords are simple—G, A Minor, C, D—a lot like Pippy's song yesterday but with a more funky feel. The chorus goes:

> And if you think it wasn't, then it was
> And if you need a reason, it's because
> I'm the riverboat captain

Maybe it's Mark Twain I'm alluding to, who ran riverboats before he wrote *Huckleberry Finn*. Or maybe it's because I need to take charge of my life, my situation with Pippy, with Celia. I feel strongly it's me I'm singing about, that I'm the riverboat captain. I wrote down the words on the back of one of the pages lying around and folded it into my shirt pocket.

The sun comes through the window in the upper corner of the basement. Celia's back home in Phoenix, probably at work by now. Last night was a night I gave up with her . . . for what? To sleep with some high school girl? I could go to jail for what I've done. There's a law against it, I'm sure of it. If there's not, there ought to be. Alex would probably tear me apart if he knew, and Gloria would come up with some clever way to kill me without ever getting her house dirty. My murder wouldn't be hard to pull off. No one knows where I am.

I'm the riverboat captain.

I hear shuffling upstairs, calm, domestic sounds. Alex must be off to work. It could be Pippy up and about, but no one's acknowledged my presence yet. The door to the rec room creaks open.

"Hote, you gonna want toast?" It's Gloria.

"Sure," I say. "I'll be up in a minute."

* * *

Gloria's smart, with an aura of professionalism that must've come from some day job or other. Like now, shuffling around the kitchen, making breakfast in a light blue workout unit unzipped to reveal a navy one-piece bathing suit underneath, her movements suggest no wasted effort. She reminds me of my mom, working the kitchen, popping bread into the toaster, never giving the slightest hint that she'd rather be anywhere else.

"Is Betty up yet?" I ask, pulling up a seat at the counter. My shower was sketchy, cheap shampoo and old soap from who knows when, and putting on dirty clothes doesn't help. I'm not entirely convinced Gloria isn't just waiting for the right moment to confront me about last night. If she does, I'll make no defense. I have none.

"She's at work," Gloria says. "She didn't tell you?"

"She must've mentioned it," I say, but I know she didn't.

"Works all day today," Gloria says. She grabs the finished toast and, with a quick gesture designed to keep her fingers from burning, drops it onto a plate. "I don't think we'll see her until five or so. Do you want peanut butter or jam?"

"Peanut butter," I say. "That blows my plan. I was hoping to catch her this morning."

"You can stop by her work," Gloria says. "She complains about her manager, but I don't think he's that bad. Here's your toast."

"Thanks," I say.

"I'd let you wait here," Gloria says. She screws the lid of the jar back on. "But I'm off to the beach as soon as the weather warms up."

The beach. I never did get my day at the ocean, waves hitting the shore, salt water drying on my face, time to reflect. "I don't suppose you'd mind if I tagged along," I say.

Gloria looks shocked, her smoothness shattered by an abrupt pause. "You want to come to the beach with me?"

"Yeah," I say.

"Won't you be late getting home?"

"I'm in no hurry."

Gloria seems to want a way out but can't think of one. She eases over to the cabinet, puts the peanut butter away. "But you don't have any swim trunks," she says.

* * *

I climb out of the clump of trees and back into the Beamer. "Here they are," I say. I open my Dart Mart bag and pull out my pair of green swim trunks.

"You weren't kidding," Gloria says.

"Bought 'em a couple days ago." I hold the trunks out in front of me. They look big enough for a giant. "I'm not going to look very stylish."

"Don't worry about it," Gloria says. She pulls out of the Equinox parking lot and turns right onto Main Street. Cars edge into the other lane. "The beach is about feeling the ebb and flow of the world around you. *It's* not taking *you* in. *You're* taking *it* in. I could never make Betty understand that."

"Betty doesn't like the beach?"

Gloria rolls her eyes, looking just like her daughter, which is the first time I've noticed any resemblance. The three of them—Betty, Alex, Gloria—remind me of the president and his family. A blond, a brunette and a red head . . . It's best not to ask questions. "If it's not Gretsches or Green Day or that Marshall stack she's always bugging me about, she's not interested."

"Yeah," I say. "She seems to have her heart set on rock 'n' roll."

"We couldn't keep her in school," Gloria says. "Conferences, therapists. No matter what we do, the girl is bound and determined to become the next Veruca Salt, except she hasn't shown any lesbian tendencies, at least not yet."

I laugh a little. "You're probably okay on the lesbian thing," I say. "Betty definitely likes guys."

Gloria flashes me a look with murder in it.

"No, I mean, not me," I say, but knowing that's not quite true either. "Listen, your daughter and I are not boyfriend and girlfriend. I don't know why she told you that. We just met each other a couple days ago and kind of liked each other, kind of had something to offer each other, and not in the way you'd think. You see, I just quit one of those bands she went to see the other night."

Gloria looks confused. Suddenly, her eyes flash. "Hong Kong Fuey," she says.

"Close enough," I say. "It's a long story why I'm sleeping in your basement, and I'd rather not get into it. What I do know is rock 'n' roll isn't what it used to be. Sure, there's still sex and drugs and people blowing their heads off, but it's mostly about writing safe, catchy pop songs and seeing how many units you can sell over the summer and Christmas seasons. For better or worse, it's lost its edge, and that bodes well for someone like you, with a daughter who's gonna rock the world come hell or high water. I've heard her songs, too; she's got talent. I know it's hard to remember with her dropping out and being a smart ass and the potential of a Marshall stack blaring away in your basement, but there's a fairly good chance Pip—I mean, Betty—will come out the other end in one piece."

Gloria eases to a stop at a red light. She looks almost ready to cry. The ramp to the interstate slants off to the right. "Thank you," she says. "Alex and I don't know what we'd do if that girl got into trouble."

"You guys shouldn't worry about her," I say. "She's got a lot of self-esteem and a really good, determined head on her shoulders. She isn't going to be taken in by just anyone."

Gloria smiles, the light turns green, and we ease onto the ramp.

"So, let me get this straight," she says. She merges onto the interstate, which doesn't look half bad now that the morning rush is over. "You met Betty at the concert two nights ago, the concert at which you were playing."

"Supposed to be playing," I say.

"You quit *before* the show?" she says. "What did your band do?"

"They played anyway," I say. "They had a fill-in."

"So, they played the concert, and you . . . "

"Slept outside."

Gloria snaps her fingers. "Which explains why your stuff is in the hedge behind the Equinox."

"It was a matter of convenience."

"So, now for the big question," she says, glancing at me. "Why'd you quit your band?"

What happened to me with Fun Yung Moon is akin to winning the lottery or being an astronaut or pitching in the World Series. To some, it's just south of being dubbed royalty. I know this because I used to feel that way. "I must be crazy, right?"

"It sounds like your band was doing pretty well."

"We did do well," I say. "But at some point you have to ask yourself, 'Is this me? Is this what I want?'"

"Well, Betty would change places with you in a second," Gloria says. "She lives and dies for bands and guitars and all that nonsense."

"Oh, come on," I say. "Didn't you dig some band in your day?"

"I don't know what you're talking about."

"Who was it? The Eagles? Zappa? The Monkees?"

"The Monkees?" she says. "Were they a band?"

* * *

The beach is on us before either of us realizes it. It's not much to look at. A quarter-moon of sand, rocks, a few people.

"Wow," I say. "There it is."

"There it is," she says.

"It seems too small to be a beach."

"Not exactly *Baywatch*," she says. The waves are breaking right up close to shore. No one's in the water. "Laguna Beach is probably more what you had in mind. We can go there if you want."

"It's okay," I say. "If this works for you, it works for me."

We pull into the parking lot. A few other cars are parked here, each one contradicting the other about the way the spaces are supposed to go. Gloria slides the Beamer up next to a set of wooden stairs that leads down to the beach.

"I brought towels for us," she says. She reaches into the back and tosses a rainbow-colored one onto my lap. "You can *changè* in here. I'll meet you down below." And she's off.

I feel a little weird changing in the car—I wish Gloria hadn't parked so close to the stairs—but I go at it like I know what I'm doing. If I'm going to get in that water, I'm going to have to scare up some courage at some point. It might as well be now.

I lay the beach towel over my waist and drop my pants to the floor, realizing a little late I have yet to take off my shoes. A few awkward moves that include a brief moment of public nudity and I'm fully in my trunks. The tie has a knot in it that seems to prevent it from working, and my pale belly loops over the waistband, but I'm in them, damn it. I'm in them and I'm ready.

The ocean air hits me as I climb down the steps. I finally smell it, ocean smell, and it lets loose chemicals in my brain. I haven't let go, really let go, in a while. There's nothing to worry about here, a beach on one hand, an ocean on the other, little clouds.

My feet squish into the sand. This beach is roomier than I thought; there's a section to the left I couldn't see from above. Three people are at that end, one flying a kite. A man with a surfboard sits on a rock, waiting for encouragement.

"Hote," Gloria yells. She's set up camp to the right. I don't want to sit down yet; I want water. I drop my towel and take off for the ocean. My feet sink into the sand with every step, but I get to the water quickly. Three splashes, *plash-plash-plash*, high-kicking to keep running for as long as I can, and I fall. It's cold underneath. A wave fights to push me back but I swim under it, popping my head up on the other side. Everyone on the beach is watching.

Another wave comes and I dive down, kicking my feet frog-like. The water gets deeper as the wave comes in, and I have to take a few strokes to reach the bottom. Rocks, shifting sand, a cloudy whiteness. The whole ground is changing, being pushed up and out and around. Everything moves as the waves dictate.

I pop my head above the surface, only to be hit immediately by another wave. I spin with it, letting it take me. The combination of fun and danger reminds me of high school, getting drunk and driving too fast, crashing some party in a neighborhood you don't know, going all the way without a condom. You never knew who was going to get hurt or arrested or in trouble. Maybe you.

The wave fizzles, and I'm left face-up in the water. The sand shifts under my hands. I immediately rescue my swim trunks, which have slid down my thighs. I knew that tie wasn't going to work. I try to re-tie it, but it's useless. So, what's the big deal? It's California. Maybe they stay on, or maybe they come off and everyone gets a show.

The breeze is cold, and I dive back in, avoiding an oncoming wave. *It's amazing how fast I could be gone from it all. One wrong move into the wrong wave, thrown headfirst into a rock*. I dive deep, a full breath in my lungs, swimming until I miss the entire wave and can see the next wave coming. *No Pippy. No Celia. No band. No guilt.* I see the blue-green curl above. *Tempt fate. You can do it. You've done it before.* I let my body float upwards. My head comes to the surface just soon enough for the wave to take me.

The effect is earthquake-like, shaking me as I'm tossed head-over-heels. A batch of water rushes up my nose, and I can't sense which way is up. I'm pulled along for what feels like minutes before the wave fizzles, and I'm left sitting in the sand again. The water escapes all around me back into the ocean. This time my trunks have migrated north, well up into my ass. I get up, adjust them. Perfect. I try to give myself to the ocean, and all I get for the effort is a belly full of water and a wedgie. There's something to be learned here, but I'm not sure I want to know what it is.

"You need a board, dude," the surfer says as I climb out of the water.

* * *

"What on earth were you doing out there?" Gloria says. She lies on her towel in her smart, navy one-piece. Her sweat suit has been folded neatly into a pillow. She wears sunglasses but still has to shade her eyes.

"What was I *doing*?" I say. I towel myself off. "I just wanted to get in."

"People drown out there all the time."

"Oh," I say, surprised, but a little proud, too.

"If you go back out, be careful," she says.

"Sure," I say. She's a mother, she can't help it. I lie on the rainbow towel, lean back on my elbows.

The surfer, perhaps inspired by me, heads into the ocean.

"Gloria," I say. "You ever think of ending it all?"

"What?" she says. I can't see her eyes through her sunglasses, but I feel her look, a tightness at her temples and forehead.

"I mean, you seem pretty settled. But did you ever, you know, come close to calling it quits?"

"Why do you ask?"

"I don't know," I say. I'd like to tell her everything, but I know I can't. I run my fingers through the sand, not looking at her. "Sometimes I'm not sure if it's all worth it."

Gloria looks up at the sun, exhales. She seems a little peeved. This isn't what she had in mind for beach talk. "Hote, I'm not going to tell you you've got it bad because you were once in a famous rock band and now you're not. It's something others want, and you don't, and that's fine. So let that be what it is." She turns on her side, takes off her sunglasses. Hints of mascara crinkle at the corners of her eyes. "But now you've got to keep one thing in mind. Your life can be anything you want from here on out. It can be good or bad, a success or failure. You can be rich, poor, married, divorced, single, gay or straight. Take your pick. But don't fool yourself into thinking it's not worth it. Despite all evidence to the contrary, people can still be truly fulfilled with their lives. It may not look like what you'd expect it to, but it's real fulfillment. You've got to find out what that is for you and go get it. It's the only way to get from the cradle to the grave in this world."

I let Gloria's words sink in. Out in the ocean, the surfer rides a wave and, for no apparent reason, falls off his board.

* * *

Gloria glides her Beamer onto her driveway. It's the middle of the day, no clouds, just sunny Southern California, the perfect place to screw up, hit rock bottom and start over again.

"Thanks for everything," I say. "I really needed that."

"Don't mention it," she says. "Where're you off to now?"

"To see Betty," I say.

"Take the car," Gloria says. She opens her door and tosses the keys back onto the seat.

"What?" I say. "You don't have to do that."

She shuts the door and leans back in through the window. "I'm not going anywhere today. You can have it all afternoon if you want."

"I couldn't," I say. I look down at the keys. Dart Mart's at least two miles away.

"Sure you can," she says, smiling.

I pick up the keys and slide into the driver's seat. I push the key into the ignition and give it a turn. The dashboard illuminates with a million digital readings. The engine's so tuned it's almost trance inducing. "You're sure you don't mind?"

"I don't mind," Gloria says. She pats the door. "Just make sure to tell Betty to come home right after work. I've got someplace I want to take her."

"Okay," I say.

"Oh yeah. Josh?" Gloria says.

"Yeah?"

"Before you go, there's one thing we have to clear up."

"What's that?"

She stands at the top of the stairs leading to her front door. She could be a teenager herself, sandy blonde hair, beach sandals, a coy look. "Remember when you asked me what my favorite band was?"

"Yeah?"

"Well," she says, "just for the record . . . Peter Frampton."

She walks through the door, and somewhere underneath the hum of the Beamer I hear the plaintive wail of a talking guitar.

Wah . . . wah-wah-wah-wah-wah.

Gloria

Breathe.

It's wrong to want to erase your family.

It's wrong to wish they never existed, to wish I'd never met Alex in that algebra class and got sucked into his logarithmic thinking. It's the way things happen when you're not paying attention. One roll in the hay with a tan California guy and you're on Spaceship Love. Alex and I got married right out of college. Both of our sets of parents rejoiced. Now I understand why.

We got right to work, Alex and I. Alex a Certified Public Accountant, I an Advertising Assistant. Sure, it wasn't something that made me delirious to get out of bed in the morning, but it was the best I could milk out of a sociology degree. I looked at the people around me—especially the people above me—at the company, and I realized this was no life. My options dwindling—infinity minus anything leaves something less than perfect—I got the positively stellar idea to have a kid.

Okay, not thought all the way through, I admit. I was still unformed clay myself, but try to tell that to someone who wants to be a mother. I thought I was smarter than the rest of them. I thought going to college made me instinctually inclined to the right decision. It turns out you still have to think about it, and sometimes that leads to an answer you might not like. No one taught me that. I skipped Thinking 101 for something that caused less friction.

Breathe.

The first six months of mommy-hood were rough, and then it was tolerable for a year, which I think was more of a reaction to it not being a nightmare anymore. Alex worked all the time. It was just me and the kid or, more accurately, it was the kid with me stumbling around the house, a mess of hormones and merlot, looking for Dr. Spock's and trying to go all day without crying.

But the kid got bigger, the baby fat went away, and I grew into something resembling the role. You learn how people expect you to act. You learn when a kid needs to be watched and when you can let it roam. You're one step ahead of them at all times. Luckily, no one ever sees you at your worst. Except the kid, of course.

That residue, that look in Betty's eye when I try to get her to do the right thing, is still there. Without a word, she tells me, "I know you're not Buddha. Don't bother putting the screws to me about anything." What I learned from college or from being married or from about a decade in advertising means nothing to her. How can you convince a kid that what feels right isn't the be-all end-all? To them, feeling right is everything. I remember the sentiment all too well. It gets you to a place I'd like to protect her from.

Through your kids you learn the vanity of it all. You learn that society means nothing, that all that matters is between your ears. I learned everything I know from raising Betty and my yoga instructor, Zenny, who paces the room among us as we practice. He reminds us to breathe. That's the best advice I have for anyone who spends a day on this earth. *Breathe.* It's amazing how easy it is to forget something as simple as that.

Surplus

Pippy's skirting work, taking a longer break than she's supposed to. Alejandro pointed me in the right direction, all the way to the back of Dart Mart, around the toy section and behind red double doors. "Tell her to get out here," he said. "Her ten minutes were up a half-hour ago."

"No one's gonna hassle me if I go back there, right?"

Alejandro shrugged. "It's like anything. Act like you know what you're doing and you'll be fine."

Pippy shoots baskets on a portable basketball hoop set up in the warehouse area. She's outfitted for work. Red Dart Mart polo shirt, red suspenders, black miniskirt, combat boots. I walk through the doors just as she tries a dunk. She gets no higher than the rim, and the ball and she come crashing to the ground.

"Hey," I say, and scurry into the room.

She sees me, her eyes dazed from impact. Her hair's in braids, which run behind her ears, like Ellie May on *The Beverly Hillbillies*. She makes no attempt to keep me from seeing her underwear—which I'm thankful she's wearing—white cotton briefs with big, orange polka dots. "I've been trying to get that shot all day," she says as I help her up. "I thought I had that last one."

"Well, take it easy," I say. "You don't need to know how to dunk to be a rock star."

"Beats work," Pippy says. She goes after the ball, which has migrated between the prongs of a forklift.

I run my foot over the cement floor. "Listen," I say. "I just wanted to apologize for—for what happened last night."

"Huh?" Pippy says. She shuffles the ball between and around her legs, Harlem Globetrotter-style.

"It wasn't right, me being older and, um, married. I should've done something to stop it."

"If you say so," Pippy says. She puts up a long shot, which clanks off the rim.

"So, I'm heading home today," I say. She's not paying attention, chasing the ball as it rolls away. "It's time for me to get back to my life." She rushes the basket for what must be another dunk, switches at the last minute to a clumsy-looking lay-up, which goes in. "I'm here to say goodbye, Pippy."

She ambles back to me. "Hote," she says. She holds the ball between her forearm and hip, a sly smile on her face. "Are you telling me you're not my boyfriend anymore?"

Almost involuntarily, I grab her by the arms, which shakes the ball loose. Her eyes startle open. "I know you have to put up this tough front all the time," I say. "I know it's important to you, but I was a creep for doing what I did with you. Anybody who does the same in the same situation would be a creep, too. It wasn't right, and I want you to hear it from me, because one day you're gonna wake up and remember that this older, married guy had sex with you when you were just a kid, and you're gonna think, 'What kind of a creep would do that to me?' I'm here to tell you that, when you think that in the future, you'll be right."

Pippy's eyes search for diversion. "What's this?" she says and grabs at my shirt pocket.

I realize too late what it is. "Hey, don't read that."

"Oh, then I definitely want to read it," she says. I try to grab it back, but she moves away. "'*And if you think it wasn't, then it was/And if you need a reason, it's because*' . . . What does this say?"

"'*I'm the riverboat captain.*' You're not supposed to see that."

"Are these song lyrics?" she says.

"They're words to a song that came to me last night. I was gonna throw it out."

"Let's play it," Pippy says, bouncing up and down. "Listen, I gotta go back to work *tout suite,* but we should hash this out tonight. Meet me at my place after work and we'll go over to Stuart's. He's my drummer."

"I won't be here," I say, shaking my head. "I gotta go home."

"Oh, quit being a baby," she says. "Your wife still thinks you're on the road, right?" She disappears out the red double doors but yells back, "And find a bass somewhere. Stuart and I don't have one."

I stand in the warehouse, stare up at the rafters. Where does she get this ability to brush off everything that gets in her way? I'm worried about going to jail, and she wants to work on new material? Events flow right through her and come back out user-friendly and easily digestible. She and rock 'n' roll will be the perfect match.

* * *

I glide Gloria's Beamer through traffic, take the left off Main Street towards Santo Domingo. The car accelerates with a serene purr. The stick shift grabs the gears with no effort. Low center of gravity, great handling, you could herd sheep with this thing.

I want to play this jam session tonight, but not for the reasons I used to want to jam. I used to want to make something as cool as the music I heard on the radio. I wanted to play that music at clubs and watch people dance or sing along. I wanted to send it to record companies with the hope of someday being heard on someone else's radio, inspiring them to do the same thing. I wanted to be part of it, part of that flow of music from one generation to the next.

But that's not why I'm going to do this tonight. With Fun Yung

Moon, I'm part of that flow. I contributed my spice to the rock 'n' roll soup, and I can go back and sample it any time I want. Now, I need to know if music has anything left for me. I wouldn't be the first guy to give it up for good. Lance had no trouble with it.

Just before the band went on the road to support *Fun Yung-Ola,* out of the blue, Lance called me.

"Hey, stranger," he said.

"Whoa," I said. His voice stunned me. There was something different about it, deep and throaty, like he'd been talking a lot since we'd last seen each other. "I didn't expect to hear from you."

"I want you to come out to see my new place in Gilbert," Lance said. "I've got some people I want you to meet."

He met me in the driveway of his house, a beige, stuccoed unit in a subdivision called the Esplanade. Lance carried a little more weight than he used to; his belly poked out of his plaid shirt, but he still walked with a swagger that said no one could take him in a game of one-on-one.

I climbed out of my truck. Neither of us knew what to say, if we should hug or not. Lance slid his hands into his shorts pockets and looked past me. "So," he said. He motioned to my pickup. "Is this what rock stars are driving these days?"

"I wouldn't know," I said. "This is what guys who still have truck payments drive these days."

"Really," he said, genuinely surprised. "I hear you guys every time I turn on the radio. You sure you're not just trying to make me feel good?"

"Gad's got all the rights," I said. "The rest of us are on salary."

"A big salary?" he asked, his eyebrows raised.

"You wouldn't be impressed."

"Well, good," he said. "I mean, not good for you, but I have to admit I wondered. Come on inside."

I met his new wife, Michelle, a narrow-hipped redhead who

greeted me at the door with a half-smile and a Corona. She carried a bundle of blankets in her arm.

"Holy shit," I said. The kid had black curly hair, just like Lance's.

"This is Artis," Lance said.

"You've got a kid, Lance."

"That I do."

"He said you'd be surprised," Michelle said. She angled Artis towards me. "Wanna hold him?"

Artis felt like a sand bag, his body rubbery, his neck wanting to pull his head this way and that. "How old is he?"

"Seven weeks," Michelle said.

"Seven weeks," I said.

"He just started sleeping through the night," Lance said. "That's why I haven't called sooner. We're just getting to the visitor stage."

"He's great, Lance," I said. I felt Artis's head in my hand. "I'm afraid I'll hurt him."

Out back, I watched Lance barbecue as Michelle put the baby to bed. Lance had changed; he'd developed this talk-y confidence that must've come from his new job, selling trucks at a car lot in Gilbert. He'd always loved talking to people, but now he took control of the conversation.

"We're gonna redo that hill so it's tiered all the way up, like a Japanese garden," Lance said, pointing with his spatula. The sun silhouetted the mountains in the distance. An evening breeze, so perfect you could believe it was manufactured right along with the house, floated through the yard. "I'm gonna put palo verdes over there, and 'Shelle wants veggies, so we'll do that. And of course, as soon as Artie's old enough, basketball court, with a dunk hoop."

"No drums?" I asked.

Lance smiled, worked the meat with the spatula. "Hote, I wouldn't do that to my worst enemy, much less my kid."

* * *

"My famous friend," Octave says as I come in. He salutes me and hops his way over, scooting around the same bass player from yesterday, who's sitting in front of the same amp. The kid sees me and breaks into the bass line for "Nickel." He smiles at me over his shoulder.

"That's pretty good," I say. "Did you guys know I was coming?"

"We were hopeful," Octave says. He stops in front of me and smiles. "What can I do for you?"

"I need a rig," I say, "but only for tonight."

"No problem," Octave says. "We've got something that'll work."

"You got a bass, too?"

Octave looks at the kid. "Pedro, give him the bass."

Pedro stands and pulls the bass strap over his shoulder.

"Listen," I say. "I don't want to be a bother. If you can't spare it—"

"It's no problem," Octave says. "Pedro just plays it when we don't need it. He's got his own bass at home."

"Oh yeah?" I say. I take the bass and throw the strap over my shoulder. Pedro's long hair is tucked up into his baseball cap. His jean jacket is fringed at the collar from too much washing. He's got this gleam in his eye, a fire that could turn into anything, depending on how things go from here. "What kind of bass do you play?"

"Hondo," he says.

"Hondo," I say. "Same as my first bass. How long you been playing?"

"Six years," he says.

I put my foot up on the amp and play the bass. It's a black, clunky thing, something in the mold of a Gene Simmons copy. The action is too high, and the strap is the kind that only adjusts so far, but it'll work for one jam. The amp, a little SWR practice amp with one twelve-inch speaker, sounds loud and crisp, and it'll be easy to transport. "I've heard you play," I say. "You're way past the Hondo stage."

"Someone needs to tell my banker that," he says.

I laugh a little. "Well . . . I feel guilty taking this one."

"No worries," Pedro says. "When you bring it back I can say I play the same bass as the guy in Fun Yung Moon."

"The guy who *used* to be in Fun Yung Moon," I correct him, "but close enough. Let's do it." I unplug the bass and pull the strap over my head. In the motion, I get a whiff of my shirt. "By the way, either of you know where I can get some clothes around here?"

* * *

On Pedro's recommendation, I spin by Manuel's Surplus in Santo Domingo. "That's the place for you," he said. I'm not sure what he meant by that, but I take his word for it.

The place does appeal to me. The bright yellow, cinder-block building takes up one corner of a lighted intersection. Half-opened windows, probably apartment windows, line the top floor, and a gravel parking lot takes up all of one side. I glide the Beamer into the lot, careful not to throw up gravel.

Inside, bare-bones shelves and racks hold Army surplus items— belts, combat boots, dungarees—plus regular worker-guy stuff like Carhardt coats and Dickies pants. Knives and compasses are underneath a glass counter where the lone attendant sits. His glasses are at the tip of his nose as he works a crossword puzzle.

It's the kind of place I used to shop during that vague period after high school when I didn't know what I was doing. The clothes are perfect for the odd job, or for a kegger in the desert. Girls liked them, too. Or so they said.

I hump it to a rack of Dickies pants and grab a pair of navy ones, 34 x 30. I'm being optimistic. I unfold the pants and hold them against my legs to see if they're long enough. "Your grandpa used to wear those," my mom said back when I wore them all the time. Her eyes sparkle when she talks of her dad. I never met him. Stroke. Gone at sixty-two. I can tell by that sparkle I would've liked him.

The Dickies shirts are long-sleeved and come in many colors—brown, blue, maroon, burnt orange—all plain, with single pockets on the front. I used to smoke back when I wore this stuff. Everybody did. Basement parties, concerts, it said who you were and what group you belonged to. It also celebrated that teenage phase when you truly didn't care if you lived or died. Living just meant you'd have to start growing up, and nobody wanted that.

I grab a chocolate brown shirt, size L, along with packs of socks and underwear, and head for the back. A saggy denim curtain passes for a dressing room door. It won't close all the way, and it only comes down to the middle of my shins, but no one's around. Unless the attendant likes to watch grown men dress, I'll be okay.

A quick undressing and redressing and I'm in my new clothes. The mirror reflects a man, young, a little haggard. I could use a haircut and a good night's sleep, but I look all right. The new clothes, fresh creases, help. Still, I feel incomplete. My wedding ring.

I hustle my booty up to the attendant, who sees me coming and puts his crossword away.

"I'd like to buy all of these clothes," I say. I set my old ones on the counter.

"Okay," he says. "What all you got?"

"Just a Dickies shirt and pants, and a pair of socks and underwear."

He gets out a calculator. "Gotta charge you for the whole packs of socks and underwear," he says.

"Do you have a place for these?" I point at my pile of dirty clothes.

The attendant looks at them, his forehead wrinkled. "Tell you what," he says. "There's a dumpster outside. You can help yourself."

* * *

It takes a while, but I eventually find my wedding ring. It was hiding next to a cluster of old Dart Mart shopping carts, the brush and dead leaves acting as perfect cover. I hold the ring up to the sunlight, look at the gold band, the etchings around the border. It's not too late. I have to believe it's not. If it is, it never meant anything. I slide the ring on.

Fife

I sat in with the Prior Angels for three gigs, right after they threw Digs out. We played local stuff while they figured out what they wanted in a new guitar player. The greatest month of my life. Pro monitor mixes, catered backstages, roadies. My family came to see us at the Amphitheater gig. After the show, my sister hit on Joel. My older brother was so jealous he wouldn't talk to me. Mom had tears in her eyes.

But in the long run they wanted to screw me. I told Joel I wouldn't throw my weight around. I'd let him lead, like he wanted. I didn't want song publishing or points or anything like that. I just wanted the gig. Joel wouldn't have it. He told me he'd only let me in if I forfeited half my gig money. "No way," I told him. "The gig money is all I have to live on." I guess that pretty much sealed my fate with the Prior Angels.

I had my own band for years, the Boulder Freaks. Everybody thought we were from Boulder, Colorado, which didn't really help us in Tempe, but we had a pretty good local following. We could play Friday nights at Richmond's when the Angels were out of town. I used to get to the gig a few hours early, just to take in the room. I liked to feel the places we played, to get a sense of the crowd and the vibe that day. I took my time setting up, tweaked the P.A., made sure everything worked. If the rest of the Freaks would've put in half the time I did it might've been a different story. Instead, Taylor teaches guitar at Milo's. Vince has two kids and installs garage door openers. Spence works at that same print shop he worked at way back when. I became the road manager for Fun Yung Moon. It was as close as I could get to being in a signed band, until now.

It's not really my kind of music, Fun Yung Moon, but hey, they don't have to know that. I grew up a Beatles fan, which means I like the melodies a little more hooky, the harmonies a little more prominent, the choruses more happy and open, but all that doesn't matter anymore. Fun Yung Moon could be Megadeth. They could be Dwight Yoakam or Foghat or Michael Jackson. I need this gig if I'm ever going to get my own thing going.

Gad and I have an understanding. I never ask for anything, and he never fucks with me. That's the way it's worked out.

He sought me out early on, right after Fun Yung Moon got signed. I worked at Berserk Records and Tapes on Mill, where I'd worked off and on since high school, managing the floor. The Freaks were in one of our many low points. Derrick, our most recent drummer, had bailed on us for a job at UPS, and I'd quit scheduling gigs until we could replace him. I was starting to entertain the idea of life without being in a band—you know, work at Berserk, keep my health insurance, have Sundays off. My problem was that I couldn't imagine life without being in a rock band. My problem now is I still can't.

Gad asked Terrence to get me from the back.

"Some guy's out front for you," Terrence said.

"Who is it?"

"How the hell should I know?"

Gad stood next to the counter, sunglasses on even though he was inside, his head cocked in a way that said he had no interest in anything but what he'd come for. His ass-length blond hair looked out of place in the nineties; pictures of Vedder and Cobain dominated the walls, and Gad looked like a throwback to the days of Skid Row.

He wore this strange, crew-neck shirt that had horizontal stripes, showing off his bony frame. I knew him from Jejune July—the worst band in the history of Tempe—but I kept that opinion to myself.

"What's up, Gad?" I said.

He slid his sunglasses down his nose. His eyes, which I'd never seen up close, were an eerie blue, hazel-y. You could see the rock star in him, the face that would sell a million records. "I hear you're the one guy in town who knows how to manage a band," he said.

True, I was known for my ass-kicking efficiency in the Boulder Freaks. Dates, equipment, prep, I covered all the bases, and that's why I went through so many sidemen. It bugged the other members that someone actually took care of business. It meant they couldn't get away with the usual bullshit, showing up late, leaving early, skimming beers from the club only to have the band pay it back at the end of the night. I told them if they were gonna be Freaks, they were gonna adhere to a code of ethics. I kept them in line, and they hated me for it.

"I know a little," I said. "Are you looking for a manager?"

"We have a manager in L.A.," he said. "Amythyst just signed us, and we're making a record this spring, but we need someone to take care of the local stuff—gigs, paperwork, whatever. I heard from a little bird you might be interested."

I'd never considered managing a band, but if that was what brought the door down, so be it. I was tired of Berserk, anyway. If Bradley asked me to work one more double shift I was going to flip. "I might be," I said.

"Of course you are," Gad said. He took out a card from the inside of his shirt sleeve. "Here's our manager's number. Call him, and he'll tell you what to do next."

"Wow," Terrence said after Gad left. "She's gorgeous. Did you get her number?"

So I played errand boy for a while. It didn't amount to much, a fax here or there, making sure the club took care of the rider, keeping a set of strings on me at all times. When the band hit the road, I was the logical choice for road manager.

Now, three years of van trips and bad meals and miles of interstate are finally paying off. Being on tour with Fun Yung Moon, I always thought I'd get a chance to meet industry people—you know, I'd be around, they'd be around—but it never worked out. Anytime some A&R guy or radio guy or publishing agent hung with the band, I was always tracking down equipment, or dealing with a club owner, or hammering the limo service for not having the car ready. You've got to stay on top of these people. It's the only way to get things done.

But this Hote thing blew the game wide open for me. The guy ditches his band and meal ticket in the middle of a tour, and I'm in the perfect position to save the day. What came over him I'll never know, but Gad won't let him back in the band, which leaves a nice vacancy. Right place at the right time. I finally understand what people mean by that.

Gad and I sat together in the back of the bus as Lookout drove us to Fresno. Even though I'd rocked in San Paolo, I still made sure Lookout got enough sleep, knowing he had an all-nighter ahead of him. I couldn't let Hote's defection slow us down. Glen was hammering me from L.A. "Someone's gotta take charge," he said. "Who's that gonna be?"

I took charge. I learned all the songs, played the gig on an instrument I hardly know, and did a pretty friggin' stellar job of it. Afterwards, I settled up with the owner, managed the load-out, and still got us on the road before midnight. I'd proven my worth, and it was time for my reward. Gad had to offer me the gig. Sure, I wasn't a real bass player, but it wasn't the time to be picky.

"You were quite the hero out there," Gad said. He smiled, handed me a Corona.

"Thanks," I said. I took the beer and wiped my brow with it. I was tired and light-headed, but I wanted to hear this. "It was fun. I think I like playing bass."

"Glad you enjoy it," Gad said, "because we're gonna need you on bass for the rest of the tour."

I was in mid-drink but I stopped. I looked at Gad over the bottle. I was about to get screwed. "The rest of the tour?" I said.

"Yes," Gad said. "It's just one more week. Then, we'll try out some people when we get home. You'll be relieved of double-duty as soon as we pick one." He must've seen my disappointment because he added, "You'll be paid, of course, as both manager and bass player."

"Oh," I said. "Great. That's good of you guys."

"I hope you don't mind playing on Hote's rig," Gad said. He stood up, picked up his gig towel and tossed it over his shoulder, like everything had been decided and there was nothing left to discuss. "I don't know if we'd be able to get anything else out here on short notice."

"Hote's rig's fine," I said. It was falling apart, right in front of me, just like it had with the Angels. I had to do something. "Listen. You got a second? I've got a proposition for you."

* * *

And that's how I sealed the deal. Sure, I still have to manage the band while we're on the road, and I'm not making any more money, but there will be no try-outs, no competitors, no other guys to take my gig away from me. I'm in Fun Yung Moon. If I have to sacrifice a little for now, well, that's just the way the game's played. It might sound like a big deal, but when those fans look up at the stage and see me, they don't know that I manage the band, or that I don't get paid for playing, or that I'm not even a bass player. They just know I'm part of this thing, part of this wall of rock 'n' roll coming at them. That's enough for now. It's going to have to be.

China Crash

Gloria meets me at her front door. I didn't even have to ring the bell. "How'd she perform?" she asks.

"Perfect," I say. "It was nice of you to lend it to me."

Gloria looks me over. "Hey, new clothes."

"Yeah, it was about time. I got this, too." I hold up the bass.

"I know," she says. "I was at Octave's. He mentioned you stopped by."

"Octave's? What were you doing there?"

"I'm not saying a word," she says. "Betty would kill me if I did."

Gloria points me to Stuart's, one house over. Circular, flat stones make a path to the front door.

"Stuart's parents aren't home from work yet," Pippy says. She ushers me down a set of stairs. "We have the place to ourselves."

Stuart's basement is tiled and mostly empty, with rugs thrown around to keep plugged-in musicians from getting shocked. In the middle of the room, on one of the rugs, sits a brand new Marshall half stack. Pippy's Gretsch leans against it. "Notice anything different?" she says. She parades over to the amp and turns with a flourish.

"The half stack," I say. "Congrats. How'd you manage it?"

"Mom and I had a little talk after work," she says. "I think Gloria's coming around."

"Well, I'm glad you finally got it," I say. "How's it sound with the Gretsch?"

"Wait and see," Pippy says. She straps on her guitar and plugs into a tuner.

Directly across from the Marshall, behind a peach sparkle drum kit, is Stuart.

No more than thirteen, Stuart has yet to experience his growth spurt. He sits shirtless on his drum throne, so bony he's almost see-through, a pair of drum sticks in his hand. His blond hair is spiked straight up, and his glasses make his eyes look too big for his face. I can tell I'd better talk first or we might be here all day. "How you doin', Stu?" I say. I walk up to him, offer my hand.

Stuart says nothing, shakes it, a small, monkey-like grip.

"Stu," Pippy says. "You don't need to be intimidated. He's very normal. Actually he's too normal."

"Hi," Stu manages.

"I hear you're quite a drummer."

This is a mistake; a compliment is something Stuart can't handle right now. His eyes get even bigger and he looks down.

"I hope you don't mind I'm a little under-watted," I say. I set my amp down in a good spot. "I only borrowed a practice amp."

"Who cares," Pippy says. "It's punk rock. We all know bass doesn't matter anyway."

"Watch it," I say, getting out my bass. "Or I'll whack you over the head with my Gene Simmons rip-off."

"Bitchin' ax," she says.

I plug the bass into the amp, the amp into the wall. I know it's crazy, but I'm kind of excited. I feel like I'm trying out for a new band. What if this is the right one, the one I've always wanted, the one that will satisfy my every rock 'n' roll urge? It's not impossible. My best rock days could still lie ahead.

I hit the power switch and try the bass. The *thud, thud* of my low E doesn't sound like it did at Octave's. I turn up the gain and "Aural Enhancer," which makes it sound a little better, but it's still not loud enough. These two are gonna blow me away. "So, Stuart," I say, seeing if the "Effects Blend" knob does anything. "You been playing drums long?"

"Um," he says. "I mean, yeah. I was—I didn't make it in fifth grade, but in sixth the good drummer went to junior high so I got first chair."

"I'm trying to scare that school learnin' out of him," Pippy says. She plugs her guitar into the Marshall.

"Stuart, how'd you get teamed up with a hoodlum like Betty, anyway?"

"Well, she's my next door neighbor," he says. "Her family's friends with my family. My mom would kill me if I didn't."

"That's good of you," I say. "Betty could use a little sympathy."

"*Sympathy for the devil,*" Pippy shouts and bangs out a bar chord. The Marshall completely annihilates all sound. Stuart yells something and throws himself into his drums.

"Hold up," I say, and they scuffle to a stop. "I'm not even ready yet."

"You're ready," Pippy says. "I heard you play something."

"Just wait," I say. I adjust the bass strap as high as it will go. It still hangs below my waist. I'll have to keep it simple. "Now," I say. "What do you two maniacs want to play?"

"New stuff," Pippy says. "Let's play your song."

"Okay," I say. I thump my bass and give my amp one last boost. "Well, the verse goes G, A minor, C, D. Like this." And I play the rhythm on the bass. It sounds thin and a little boring, but I stick with it.

Pippy plays bar chords. "Play them open," I say. "You're making it sound like metal." She snarls and turns down her amp. She tries again, the chords coming full and clean.

"Great," I say.

Stuart keeps a steady beat, but he goes to his rack of roto-toms at the end of every progression. "Stuart, forget the rotos," I say. He does, and the groove gets going. I have a strange authority over these two. It's the kind of power that could corrupt me, but it feels good; for once they have to listen to me.

The progression sounds untamed, but it's coming together. Pippy wants to break free—just like Digs—the Marshall crackling under the scrape of her chords. It feels soothing in a way, all that power ready to erupt. Stuart pops the drums. The rattle of ghost notes between snare hits reminds me of Bonzo, of Keith Moon. *Ghosts. Ghosts are everywhere in here.*

"Okay," I say. "Here's the chorus." I play the chorus, a simple progression—C, B, A minor, B—over and over again. It takes Pippy a second to get it; she's never played a B where you adjust one finger from the C chord, but after a few times around she's doing it. Stuart goes to the ride cymbal, making the difference between verse and chorus clear. It's flowing. There's rock happening in this room.

I jump to the D at the end of the chorus and go back to the verse. There's no P.A., so I sing the words as loud as I can into the room.

> Curtain up
> Keep it straight
> You know that I won't hesitate to walk away from you

Pippy smiles at me, trying to make me self-conscious. I give her the finger and sing louder.

> Ante up
> Place your bets
> I'll be the one with no regrets and no complaints

We're grooving, and I nod to the others. My voice sounds funny, like I'm screaming instead of singing, but I don't care. I'm among friends, the living and the dead. Here comes the chorus.

And if you think it wasn't, then it was
And if you need a reason, it's because
I'm the riverboat captain

Stuart misses coming back into the verse, screwing us all up for a second, but we get rolling again.

Stay in touch
Don't run and hide
You know that I put things aside to keep them beautiful

Pippy gets cocky, playing the D chord higher up on the neck.

Way to go
And way to be
You know that I can't make you see what isn't there

Again I nod; the chorus comes, and my band's right there with me.

We'll pass oranges with our necks just like *Charade*
And with our drinks we'll all make lemonade
Cuz I'm th–

"Wait," Pippy yells.

Everyone stops playing. Pippy stares at me with a combination of shock and amusement. "What are you singing?"

The weird pre-chorus. I knew it'd be a tough sell. "It's from a movie called *Charade*. There's this scene where they pass oranges with their necks."

"So, you felt the need to put that in your song?"

"Just play, Pippy."

We run through the second chorus to the bridge, and I stop them. "Okay," I say, "this part requires some *cojones*. Pippy, here are the chords." I play them for her—G, A minor, C, G—with a stop the third time around on the A minor. She gets them, but she gets confused coming back out of the bridge. "It's some kind of weird C," I say. "It might be C-seven." She tries it. "That's it," I say. "Now, let's do the whole thing from the end of the chorus, and Stuart, don't be afraid of those cymbals."

"Should I use the china?" he asks. He points to the china crash cymbal behind him.

In the mid-1980s, drummers started getting china crash cymbals with their drum kits, and the rest of us haven't been the same since. Its loud, shrill tone is enough to make you sterile. "Save the china," I say. "Maybe we'll use it later."

We bang through the bridge. Stuart eats up the chance to work the cymbals. Pippy kicks up the volume. We're ragin', the three of us, full-on. We go straight to the last verse.

> Belly up
> But stay the course
> You know they'll all come out in force to see the tragedy

Pippy plays at top volume, and Stuart follows suit, working the cymbals twice as often as he should. I don't have the heart to stop them. I've complained enough already. Rock 'n' roll goes fast and loud until it doesn't go anymore. I sing the last chorus, even though no one can hear me.

> And if you think it isn't, well it is
> And if they never call, hey, that's the biz
> Cuz I'm the riverboat captain

We're rocking, and it all comes back to me; the night Lance and I first heard "Hey, Hey, What Can I Do" by Led Zeppelin, cruising around in his dad's Cutlass, pulling over because we didn't want to miss a second of it; Digs announcing at Richmond's that he'd said his final fuck you to the Prior Angels; breaking up with my girlfriend and listening to *Zen Arcade* over and over again; skipping senior prom to see Stevie Ray; blowing off class when the Replacements were in town; coming to work late after a night at a Prior Angels gig. I remember living it, that simple, human pulse. All of my favorite bands are right here, right here in this song, and I'm here with them.

The three of us spin out of control. I play chords on the bass—G, A minor, C, D—my volume tapped; bass chords are the only way I can make more noise. We slow through the last progression, and right at the end, just where I imagined all the instruments crescendoing to a sweet finality on the G, Stuart, with a smile that radiates all the mischief in the world, smashes the china crash cymbal, ending our jam with a shrill, if brilliant, mistake.

Stuart

Tollar'll never believe it. A rock star in my house, jamming with Betty and me, plugging his amp into the wall just like anyone and playing that weird looking bass. Tollar can brag about his SVT and his Rickenbacker and his trip to the Rock 'n' Roll Hall of Fame. Hell, Tollar. I've got the real deal right here.

I run up the stairs. He wants to leave, so I offered him a Coke to stall him. I've got to get proof. I can't let it end like it did with Sammy Hagar, forgetting to get his autograph. "Oh, you just ran into him," Tollar said the next day. "You just ran into Sammy Hagar at the Angels game, and we're supposed to believe it." Tollar can be such a dick.

My camera, the one Grandma got me for my birthday, is in my bedroom somewhere. "It's got a timer so you can take pictures of yourself playing drums," Grandma said. "Doesn't that sound like fun?" No, but taking pictures of Betty in her swimming suit does. Not that any of them turned out. I was too far away, and laughing the whole time.

I get to my bedroom and pull open my dresser drawer. Baseball cards. Shimano hub. My yellow belt. It's not here. What did Mom do with it?

You never know what this could lead to. Hote's from the big time, he's got connections. Those kids on TV forming their own band, they had to come from somewhere. And the youngest Backstreet Boy was about my age when they started. Maybe Hote's scouting for talent, to play songs and make CDs and tour all over the country. I'd do that, as long as I can be home before soccer starts.

My backpack hangs from a hook in the closet. I open it and—excellent!—the camera's in the front pocket. But it's too light. When I turn it over I see why. No film. Shit. There's no way they'll take me to the store.

"Stuart," Betty yells upstairs. "Hote's leaving."

It's an autograph or nothing. I go to my desk and snag a Sharpie and a sheet of paper. Wait. Their CD. I find it in my rack, *Fun Yung Wah!*, towards the bottom. I haven't listened to it in a while, and then only that one song. I'll listen to it all the time now.

When I get back downstairs, all of his gear is packed. Betty's got him cornered by her Marshall, totally flirting with him. "Hote," I say, getting between them. "Can you sign this? The kids at school aren't gonna believe it."

The Good Morrow

Practice is over. Stuart's parents are due home any minute, and I don't want to be around when they get here. Stuart asked me to sign his copy of *Fun Yung Wah!* and immediately dashed upstairs, probably to see how much he can get for it on Ebay.

Pippy and I go out the side door to the driveway.

"So, what exactly did you do to my mom?" she asks.

"Huh?"

She ambles towards me, her tongue tracing the inside of her lips. "She only agreed to buy the amp because of something you did, I'm sure of it. Did you two hook up or something?"

"What?" I say. "Pippy, it's your mom."

"Well," she says. "She's happy all of a sudden. What am I supposed to think?"

"Not that."

"Then what happened?"

"I just told her the truth," I say. "I told her that being in rock music isn't some guarantee you'll become a suicidal, crack-smoking egomaniac, but then again nothing would guarantee you wouldn't. I told her I thought you'd be challenged by things, but that I thought you were up to the task, and when it was all said and done you'd come out the other end just fine."

"Oh," Pippy says. She smiles and—for the first time in three days—blushes.

"It's the truth," I say. "Nothing's guaranteed because you've got talent, but I think you're gonna get an opportunity, and you're gonna Pippy-fy it, and rock 'n' roll will be the better for it."

She won't look at me. Her hands are behind her back, her head down. If I didn't know better I'd say she was embarrassed.

"Now, I was hoping you could do something for me."

"What?" she says.

"Actually, I need you to do three things for me. First, I need you to take back the equipment I borrowed from Octave. I told him I'd get it back to him as soon as possible, and I'm not gonna be here."

"Easy," Pippy says. "What else?"

"While you're at Octave's," I say. "I want you to listen to Pedro play."

Pippy looks confused. "Who's Pedro?"

"He's the bass player who sits in there and plays all day."

Pippy's eyes fill with horror and she backs up. You'd think I asked her to go to a Damn Yankees concert. "No way," she says.

"Just listen to him," I say, "and think about taking him into your band."

She wiggles in a way that reveals her disgust. "He's a metalhead," she says.

"And he's the best bass player you'll hear in this town," I say. "You need him. Trust me."

She crosses her arms, turns away with a pout. I should've saved Pedro for last. "Okay," she says. "But I only promise to consider it."

"That's all I'm asking," I say.

A cargo van turns at the head of the street. I'm afraid it's Stuart's parents, but it glides by. It's time for me to go.

"There's one last thing," I say.

"What?" she says, still not looking at me.

"It's the most important one of all."

"You're getting a lot already."

"I know," I say, "but this one's important. I want you to promise me you won't become a suicidal, crack-smoking egomaniac. And not because I told your mom you wouldn't, but because you're worth a lot more than that. And I'd kick myself if you *do* become a suicidal, crack-smoking egomaniac and I didn't do something about it while I had the chance."

* * *

I'm back at Dart Mart. The parking lot teems with cars and people. A landscaper mows the lawn out front using a new kind of riding mower that you stand on. Dusk has settled in; it'll be dark soon.

I pick up the pay phone and dial Celia's number. My legs are tired. I walked here from Stuart's. Pippy offered to give me a ride, but I didn't want one. I felt I should clear my mind of everything, a nice break between the last few days and what comes next. I retrieved my Dart Mart bag from the trees, my anthology, the Prior Angels CD. It's all I'm taking home with me.

I flip through the book while the phone rings. I stop at "The Good Morrow," the poem that links me to my college days with Celia. The little doodles are great, hearts, peace signs, declarations of love only we would ever see. I want to go back there, back to when Celia and I first fell for each other. I'd skip everything in between, if only I could. I'd forgive everything, too.

The phone rings and rings, and I hear it forward to her voice mail. *You've reached Celia at Phoenix Business Magazine* ... Do I leave a message? We need to talk face-to-face, but I should let her know to expect me. The greeting ends on a quick *beep*.

"It's me," I say. "I'm sorry I haven't called sooner. I'm in San Paolo, hoping to catch a flight home. It's getting late so it's probably gonna be tomorrow." A car idles by. The guy behind the wheel stares at me. I turn away. "I've spent the last few days trying to figure things out. I can't say I totally get it, but I know one thing for sure. I want

us back. I want you back, Celia." I look down at the book. My thumb
marks the page with the poem. "I was just reading something that
brought back a lot of memories, and I wanted to read it to you, to see
if you remember it.

> "I wonder, by my troth, what thou and I
> Did till we loved? Were we not weaned till then,
> But sucked on country pleasures, childishly?
> Or snorted we in the seven sleepers' den?
> 'Twas so; but this, all pleasures fancies be.
> If ever any beauty I did see,
> Which I desired, and got, 'twas but a dream of thee."

I'm filled with the pulse of the words, a warmth that gives me
goosebumps. Just like music.

> "And now good-morrow to our waking souls,
> Which watch not one another out of fear;
> For love all love of other sights controls,
> And makes one little room an everywhere.
> Let sea-discoverers to new worlds have gone,
> Let maps to others, worlds on worlds have shown,
> Let us possess one world, each hath one, and is one."

One world. Celia and me.

> "My face is in thine eye, thine in mine appears,
> And true plain hearts do in the faces rest;
> Where can we find two better hemispheres
> Without sharp north, without declining west?
> Whatever dies, was not mixed equally;
> If our two loves be one, or thou and I
> Love so alike that none do slacken, none—"

Beep. Her voice mail cuts me off. I won't call back. She'll get the rest from me tomorrow. "None can die," I say and hang up.

"Need a ride?"

It's the guy who just idled by. He stands in front of his rusted-out car, which barely acknowledges its parking space. He's tall, his frame bent like a yardstick cracked in the middle.

"No," I say. "Thanks, anyway."

The stranger doesn't move. "Were you gonna call a cab or something? You don't need to. I'll take you wherever you wanna go."

"Why would you do that?"

"I don't know," he says. He laughs a little. "Trying to do you a favor, I guess."

"Thanks all the same." I head towards the Dart Mart entrance. I have no place else to go, and it offers safety until this guy clears out.

"Josh," he says.

He knows my name? How does he know my name?

"I'm your dad."

I turn. He's frozen by his car, a cigarette burning in one hand. The hair, the eyes, it could be my dad, and it scares the shit out of me. "Listen," I say. I take a few steps towards the store. "I've got some things to pick up in here." I take off, not running but moving quickly.

"I'm not goin' anywhere," he says. "I've been waitin'—I'm not goin' anywhere."

The doors open, and I hustle through them. My heart beats heavily. In a way, it feels like I've been waiting for this my whole life, but in another way it feels like it never has to come, like it shouldn't. The Dart Mart men's room sits off to the right. I push through the door.

To my surprise, the interior of the men's room is a deep blue, debunking every guess I could make about a Dart Mart restroom. There's no one else here. The three chrome stalls and three sinks are all unused.

I go to a sink. My dad—someone who says he's my dad—is in the parking lot, waiting for me, and I'm hiding in the bathroom. I don't know what to say to him. I don't even know him. I lean on the sink, breathe in the scent of Dart Mart soap.

I look into the mirror—which isn't a mirror at all but a mirror-like piece of metal, scratched and dented. The damage doesn't prevent me from seeing my face. So, here's real life—not some fantasy I've dragged with me from my adolescence but real life with real complications and a real dad. No more skating around adulthood, hoping no one notices I have yet to commit. It's arrived, and I guess that means I've arrived with it.

I go back outside. The man who calls himself my dad leans against the hood of his car, smoking a cigarette. When he sees me, he stands up straight.

"You're a lot bigger than I thought you'd be," he says.

"What's my mom's first name?" I'm on the Dart Mart side of the traffic lane. I'm not going over there until I know for sure.

"What?" he says. His eyes look detached, like two moons orbiting the planet of his head. A car eases between us. "Your mom's name is Sally."

I pace along the curb. "That was an easy one," I say. "What town is she from?"

"How many of these do I have to get right?"

"I don't know yet," I say. "I'll let you know when you get there."

He leans against his car again, takes a pensive drag of his cigarette. "Montreau," he says. He blows smoke out his nose. "Sally's from Montreau, Illinois."

I stop pacing, look at him. He's calm, unrattled. There's a very real possibility I'll be hugging this guy in a minute, but I can't let him off without a hard one. There's one detail I happen to know that only my dad would know, too. "What was the name of the restaurant where you two worked together?"

He smiles. "That's a good one," he says. "Willohby's. I fell for Sally, your mom, at Willohby's."

I look at him, and tears bubble in my eyes. "Well, what the hell are you doing here?" I say. I come across the lane and hug him, feel my dad underneath my hands, and he feels me.

"You look like your Uncle Randy," he says. He pulls himself away, chases away tears like they're bugs that bite him. "I remember Randy had these big hands. Did your mom ever tell you about my family?"

"Not really," I say. "She said you didn't get along with them."

"That's not true," he says. He drops his cigarette and mashes it out with his foot. "I used to get on with Randy. I don't know why she told you that."

"I think she was talking about your mom and dad and stuff."

"Well," he says. "We didn't always see eye-to-eye, but we got on all right. Once you were born, we didn't go over there much because Dad and me . . . Listen, it's a long story. You want a ride somewhere? I can take you anywhere."

The passenger's seat swivels so you can get in the back more easily. "This is the only car that does this," he says, demonstrating it for me. He tosses a phone book and some clothes into the back seat.

"Nice El Camino," I say.

"*Grand Torino*," he corrects me. I get in, and he shuts my door. A plastic cup is lodged between the seat and the emergency break. An empty vial, the kind for prescription pills, rattles around by my feet. The car smells of cigarettes.

Dad climbs into the driver's side. "So, where to?"

"The airport," I say. "I'm going home."

"Homeward bound," he says. He starts the car—a loud, throaty *RRrrr*—and pops the stick shift into gear. We idle up to Main Street.

"So, how'd you find me?" I ask.

"I stopped by your mom's the other day. She put me on your tail."

"Wow," I say. I try to imagine the two of them in the same room. I'm glad I wasn't there.

"So, I've been trolling around this club you played," he says, "and I saw you talking on the phone and thought, 'I wonder if that's him?'" He looks at me and smiles, a crooked-toothed grin, and I can't help but smile back. It hits me that, not only are we related, we could actually like each other.

A long line of cars, half with their headlights on, heads south, coming home from the city. We turn north.

"We're lucky to be going this way," I say. "Do you know where the airport is?"

"No," he says, then points to the sky. "I'm following those planes. Did you know that? You can find the airport in any city just by following the planes." He lights another cigarette, holding the steering wheel with his thighs. "Anything you want to know about me?"

"I don't remember much," I say, which isn't true. The truth is I don't remember anything about him. "Mom says you were a cook at Willohby's and you guys—you two had a fling." I don't like talking about this. No one should have to talk about their mother having a fling with anyone, ever. There are no rules to this game, or no one has taught them to me. "She told me not to be mad at you. She said she was the one who ran off."

"That's your mother for you," he says. He shakes his head. I think he's angry. I feel like everything I say sets him off in a direction I can't quite follow. "I mean, she had her reasons—you'd never hear me say she didn't—but she has a way of glorifying herself." He looks at me and back at the road. "Your last name's Phillips, or at least it should be. There's nothing wrong with being a Hotle—if that's what you want—but you're a Phillips."

I don't know want to say, but I have the feeling I shouldn't say anything. We cruise past a little green sign with a plane on it. "Hey," I say. "I think the airport's next."

"Is it?" he says. "Good eye."

"It's pretty amazing you found it," I say. "I didn't even know Orange County had an airport."

"Did you fly a lot with the band?" he asks.

"Not much anymore. They used to shuttle us all over the place—Chicago, Dallas—but no one's playing the new record."

"You guys make any money?"

He laughs, but he's serious, too. Again, not something I want to get into with him. There seems to be a whole list of things we can't talk about. "I got by," I say. "But I'm out now. I'll have to find another way to make a living."

"Remember," Dad says. He leans closer to me. His eyebrows are bleached from the sun. "You can always find money. Take me, for instance. Your dad might not look like much—kind of a tramp, right?—but ever since I was old enough to work I've had a ten-dollar bill in my pocket. I don't know how much happier you can be than that."

"You seem happy enough," I say, not sure if he really does or not.

"I am," he says. "There's nothing out there I want that I can't get."

"What do you do for work?"

"Little of everything," he says. "Don't believe those people who say you have to do one thing. Early on I worked in kitchens. I cooked at a casino in Vegas. I lived in Mexico for two years. I guess you could say I'm between jobs right now."

"Me, too." We both laugh.

The airport sign points us to the right. "Here's the turn-off," I say.

The road divides and Dad takes the lane for outgoing passengers.

Signs for airlines hover overhead. "You can drop me anywhere," I say. "I don't know which one I'm taking, so it doesn't matter."

"You don't have a ticket?"

"Not yet."

He idles to the curb, shifts to park. "Then why don't you let me drive you home?" he says. "I'm headin' east, too."

We circle back towards the interstate, Dad and me, and this time we get stuck in the line of traffic we managed to avoid on the way here. The other cars are filled with teachers, lawyers, business people, all ending their work week with a long commute home. They'll be greeted by families and pets and two full days off once they get there. The idea of such a life used to scare me, but I don't feel that way right now. I feel like one of them, a kid in a car with his dad, freshly picked up from school or soccer or piano, edging towards home. I can imagine the peace I'll feel once I get there.

* * *

Dad and I talk all the way home. I tell him about high school, how sports were a waste of time and how I took to music instead. He tells me that music runs in our blood, that he and Randy used to sing in the choir when they were kids, that he wishes he would've stuck with it. I tell him how Fun Yung Moon once opened for Johnny Cash, and how I met Alice Cooper backstage at one of our shows. He tells me about New Orleans and juke joints and the dope you could buy right on the street. I tell him I don't do drugs. "That's good," he says. "Keep it that way."

He tells me he doesn't get the way people live now, that everybody worries too much. He'd gladly trade every cell phone and new car and 401k for one night with everyone having a good time. I tell him I haven't had a good time in a long time. "We gotta change that," he says.

He pulls over at a truck stop in Blythe and buys an Allman Brothers cassette. We sing the choruses together the rest of the way to Phoenix.

It's after midnight when we pull up to my house. The mesquite tree in the front yard is completely leafless. I'll be raking tomorrow.

I climb out, Dart Mart bag in tow. Dad comes around to my side, crosses through his headlights and briefly causes the houses up the block to disappear.

"You gonna be okay?" he asks. I explained Celia's and my situation to him. He was polite enough to listen and wise enough not to say anything.

"We'll be fine," I say. "Now that I'm home maybe we can start over."

"I'm headin' home, too," he says. "I'm gonna try to pull some things together, see what happens, but I'm thinking about moving down here next year." He runs a hand through his hair. The street lamps give him a young, lean silhouette. James Dean. "Would you like that?"

"You bet," I say, and I hug him.

I feel the jerks of what must be sobs coming from him, and he pulls away.

"Great," he says. He heads back to his side of the car. "I don't have a phone right now, but I'm gonna get one, and when I do you can have the number."

"Cool," I say.

He stops before he gets in his car, looks at me, smiles. "I don't know why I always thought you'd be smaller," he says. He drives off, the Torino chugging into the night.

No lights are on at the house, not even the porch light. In the driveway free newspapers sit, the Buy Rite and others. I grab them, shake off the mesquite leaves.

The front entryway is dark. It's hard to find my key. Celia will be asleep, but I'll have to wake her. There are so many things I have to tell her. I have a dad; I quit the band; I've been unfaithful; I'm sorry. It's late. Maybe I should keep it simple. I love you. That's all she needs to know tonight.

I find the key, turn the knob. The place smells of dust. Our house opens to a room we rarely use, the dining room. The living room and kitchen are farther back, where all the real action happens, and the bedrooms are off to the right. I hit the overhead light in the dining room. Chandelier, painting, bleached-wood table and chairs. On the table sits a folded piece of paper. I see my name, "Josh," written on one side of it. I pick it up.

Josh,

I've gone someplace to be alone, to think things through. The more I thought about it, the more I couldn't stomach facing you. I'm sorry for what I've done, but I don't know if that's enough. A spell has been cast over us, and I cast it, and I get sick thinking I might not be able to summon it away.

Please don't worry about me. I'll figure it out, and I'll come back to you.

Love always,
Cel

I read the note again. *Someplace to be alone . . . couldn't stomach facing you . . . sorry for what I've done.* What *she's* done. Good god. If she only knew.

I feel the weight of her absence, and it forces me to sit down. I'm stuck alone in this house, without her, and I can't stand it. I drop my head to the table, let the tears flow. She thinks she's the only one at fault. She's not. I'm more at fault than anyone. It's almost fitting, after what I've done, that I'm the one who has to wait.

June 1996

The Attic

I wish I could say things happened differently. I wish I'd never made my mistakes and that Celia'd never made hers. I wish life was easy and pleasurable and uncomplicated. I wish Hüsker Dü were still together. I wish rock 'n' roll lasted forever.

I tried to explain it to Brandon. We hung out together one night in my back yard. Spring had sprung. The flowers of the saguaro cacti bloomed, yellow and waxy. It had been months since I'd come home, a full Thanksgiving and Christmas and New Year's without Celia. I still haven't heard from her.

Brandon had started coming over after I put the house up for sale. He's the realtor's kid, not to mention the biggest fan of Fun Yung Moon you'll ever meet. When he heard that his dad represented someone from the band, he started making excuses to come by, adding a lock box, changing the sign out front, "just checking in." At twenty-two, Brandon should've been out chasing girls, but he was more interested in hanging out with me on my back patio, smoking cigars and talking about music. I guess I liked his company.

Brandon's a smart, good-looking kid, with inquiring brown eyes and slicked-back hair. It's a style that's beyond me. It looks fine on him, but I lump it in with other disturbing nineties fashions, like pro sports gear and baggy jeans worn well below the ass.

"It infuriates me you guys aren't rich and famous," he said. He took a drag from his cigar. Brandon not only thinks our follow-up record, *Fun Yung-Ola,* is better than our debut, *Fun Yung Wah!* He thinks it's better than just about anything else. I'm flattered, but mostly I'm concerned. *Fun Yung-Ola* died shortly after I left the band. I don't think they even made it back out on the road.

"Wasn't meant to be," I mumbled. I dropped an ash into the stand-alone, bronze ashtray. Brandon always brought cigars, Cohibas and Montecristos and El Rey Del Mundos. He spent more money on them than he ought to. I tried to get him to stop, but he wouldn't listen.

"That's just not true," he said. "I saw you when you first started out. You had the songs, the show. You guys were the epitome of 'meant to be.' What happened?"

I exhaled some smoke, set my cigar down. "First of all," I said, "we threw our drummer out. Then, some people got big heads. Others did too many drugs. We trusted each other too much in the beginning, then not at all in the end. We made too much money—or not enough money—depending on how you look at it. We grew apart, Brandon. That's about the sum of it. The better question is 'How did we get as far as we did?'"

Brandon shook his head, took a tug from his cigar. He stared off into the distance, the mountain, the night. "I'll never understand it," he said.

"Yes, you will," I said. I got up from my chair, dusted some ash off my pants. "I'm having another beer. You want one?"

* * *

The first nights alone were the hardest. Eating dinner by myself, staying up too late, going to sleep in bed sheets that still smelled of her. Loneliness kept pinching me, rousing me to futile tasks, chasing me from one room to the next. Her clothes I left untouched in the closet. Her almost-empty shampoo bottle never made it to the trash. I lost weight, quit shaving. One phone call from her would've ended it.

But it never came. A week, a month, two months. It was like she'd forgotten me, forgotten her life, her promise to come back. No one from her work knew where she went, what her plans might've been. "She didn't talk about any of that," Patti the receptionist said. "She kept her cards close to her chest. I always thought she was perfect."

"She was," I said and hung up the phone.

I convinced myself I was the problem. I held her back, diminished her, brought her down to earth when she could've just as easily floated away.

Maybe that's what she did, I thought. Maybe Celia quit this world, vacated it for a better, more sacred place. Fine. I could live with that. As long as I could imagine her somewhere perfect, I had no pain. Come back to me, or disappear forever. Nothing but the truth, that solid middle ground between dreams and the waking present, could hurt me.

"Divorce her," my mom said. We were celebrating my twenty-seventh birthday. Mom went out of her way to try and cheer me up, decorated the townhouse, baked a cake. "She doesn't deserve you. There are plenty of other women out there. What are you waiting for?"

"I don't know," I said. I flipped through my birthday present, an anthology of Beat literature. "Celia still might come back. She said she would."

Mom put her hand on mine, stopped me from twiddling the pages. "But she hasn't, honey," she said. Tears formed in her eyes, the eyes of a woman who'd run away once herself, eyes that knew. She backed away, wiped her face. "And if she does, why on earth would you want her?"

"She's not the only guilty party," I said, but it doesn't matter. She's my mom. It's her job to look past my faults. What more could I ask of her?

Dad's another story. As abruptly as he appeared, he fell off the face of the earth again. I haven't heard from him since the night he dropped me off, which somehow surprises me even more than Celia. He seemed so ready for a change. He talked about how he wanted to settle down, how he hated Oklahoma City . . . But he's a wanderer; you can't forget that. How can you argue against freedom?

Gad called me shortly after New Year's. I'd heard nothing from him, or from anyone else in the band. I wondered when he might call. I knew he'd want a clean break, no ambiguity.

"There's some paperwork coming your way," he said. "It's similar to what we did with Lance. You own nothing, but this document makes sure you don't change your mind."

"Whatever," I said.

"Unfortunately," he said. He was taking more pleasure in this than he cared to admit. "Unlike when we threw Lance out, there's no money in the coffers, so we have nothing to offer you for severance."

"That's fine," I said. "I'm not asking for anything."

"And you're out," he said. "You're out of Fun Yung Moon, in case that doesn't go without saying."

"It goes without saying."

There was an uncomfortable silence. I looked at my hand on my leg, folded in all my fingers, save one.

"Well?" he said. "Do you have anything to say?"

"Like what?"

"Like that you're sorry," he said. "Like that you regret how it ended." He paused. I could hear him at the other end of the line, a faint change in the buzz, a hesitation. "Like that you miss it and want to come back."

I closed my eyes, rubbed my fingers over them, little sparks flying in the dark. "Nope," I said. "Nope. I can't say any of that."

"Good," Gad said. "It's good you go away with a clear conscience. Fife will be calling you this week about getting your rig back."

"Tell him he can keep it."

"What?" Gad said.

"I can always get another bass," I said. "And I stole that amp in the first place."

"That was decades ago," Gad said. "And you paid Sammy back in full."

"I paid back the money," I said, "but I never gave the amp back. This way I don't take away anything that I didn't give back."

"You're being a martyr," Gad said, getting mad. "You're caught up in the romance of sacrifice."

"Maybe," I said. "Either that or I'm sacrificing. Take your pick."

A few weeks later, after the house sold for more than anybody thought possible, I heard a knock at the front door. No one was there, but sitting on the patio was the black case of my bass guitar. I got it inside and opened it. There it was, my tobacco Fender, bronze pick guard, rosewood neck. It looked like someone had cleaned it, polished the tuning pegs, run a shammy over the body. I picked it up and played the first thing that popped into my head, a Stevie Wonder lick, the one from "Sir Duke." Then I played "The Lemon Song" by Led Zeppelin. Then I played "Livin' Lovin' Maid." I jammed all afternoon, remembering songs, playing as many of them as I could until I couldn't remember any more. Music. It's part of me. I shouldn't have given it up so easily. "Thanks, Fife," I muttered as I put it away.

* * *

I left Phoenix in April, the day the house closed, just as the sun was starting to bake me through the windshield of my truck. I drove west on I-10, going the opposite direction that my dad and I had driven six months previously. I had to resist taking the Orange County exit, to go and see how Pippy was doing. I'd see her soon enough, on MTV or whatever, at a good, safe distance.

I turned north instead, up Highway 101, and ended up in San Francisco. I rented an apartment on California Street, as close to North Beach as I could get. I'll apply to all the colleges next year.

The money from the house sale won't last forever, which means I'll have to get a job. I wonder what that will be like.

And when I miss Phoenix, I think of what I left behind. Not Celia or Fun Yung Moon. I mean what I literally left behind. Up in the attic of the house, behind a vent tube and a piece of insulation that no one would ever think of moving, a cubby hole extends above the garage. Inside, protected from weather and people and natural disaster, I left four things—my Prior Angels CD, my anthology of English literature, my bass and, in the fur-lined compartment of the bass's case, my wedding ring, wrapped in a shammy, waiting for me if, someday, I want it back bad enough to go get it.

The author would like to thank Raquel Edwards and Lewis Buz-
bee, both of whom offered unfailing encouragement and a keen
critical eye during the writing of *Ghost Notes*.

Great care has been taken to ensure that *Ghost Notes* is free of
typos, misspellings, omitted words and errors of fact. How-
ever, if you should happen across one of the above, please let
me know at art@artedwards.com, and I will correct it in the
next version.

Art's first solo CD, *Songs from Memory*, which includes the single
"Riverboat Captain," is available at www.artedwards.com.

Ghost Notes Version 1.0 October 2007

Printed in the United States
205518BV00001B/20/A

9 780979 906619